Heartbreak & Restoration

Mission: To Proclaim Transformation and Truth

Publisher: Transformed Publishing, Cocoa, FL
Website: www.transformedpublishing.com
Email: transformedpublishing@gmail.com

ISBN: 978-1-953241-31-3 Paperback

Heartbreak & Restoration

He Rescues Me

Imani Gillespie

Dedication

I dedicate this book first and foremost to God Himself. Thank You for Your never-ending grace, Your ever-so-patient Love, and Your heartfelt kindness toward me. Thank You for loving me wholeheartedly, before I knew how to love You back. Thank You for Your patience with me as I learn how to love and trust You with *all* my heart. Thank You for mending a heart You didn't break, over and over again.

Next, I dedicate this book to every reader who is on their own journey of healing and self-discovery. It is for you that I have experienced what I have, to acknowledge with you that hurt does hurt. I am here to provide a safe space where we can verbalize how devastating emotional pain can be. My story will reassure you that there is always purpose in the pain, even when all seems so blurry. With me, you will explore the new perspective that God really is in it all. Truth be told, every experience has treasure to be found within it - liberation through honesty with yourself and God, healing from what has stunted the evolution of your family through confrontation, mourning and/or celebrating with one another, rediscovering yourself or rebuilding yourself anew. These are all beautiful things that may be awarded to you in the process of feeling blue.

Lastly, I dedicate this book to my cousin Twonnie. When I lost you, I lost me. The fact that you didn't get the chance to be all I believe you were destined to be in this lifetime because of gun violence in our community, challenged me to pull myself out of depression and continue to pursue my dreams. I promised you I wouldn't let this cycle of dysfunction and devastation continue. You challenged me, in spirit, to start with me - *"Can't help anybody else out unless I'm free."* Thank you for existing, inspiring, motivating and always showing love to everybody you encountered with your goofy self! The memory of you still carries me.

Preface

In fact, everyone who wants to live a godly life in Christ Jesus will be persecuted,

-2 Timothy 3:12

Thank you for willingly embarking on this journey of witnessing my imperfections. I pray that through them, you may see God's perfection. This process of purification has been years in the making. There is still so much I need God to cleanse me from and heal me of. Yet, as I lay in bed reflecting, I am in amazement of the works of His hands; seeing where I came from, to where I now am.

This Christian walk is not easy, clean cut, or pristine. The beauty is, that's exactly why He sent Jesus, *"... It is not the healthy who need a doctor, but the sick. I have not come to call the righteous, but sinners."* (Mark 2:17 NIV). The desires I've felt ashamed about, the thoughts I intentionally keep hidden, the habits that have brought death to my heart and body— these are the things Jesus delights in making clean. He's not afraid of my dirt. That's one of the most comforting things I've learned.

This has been a laborious, uphill battle: living in a cycle that flows in between two worlds constantly – awe and anguish, triumph and tragedy, Love and loss. My life is a never-ending process of purification through the operation of what is essentially a spiritual open-heart surgery. I am becoming holy by courageously confronting my truth, time and time again, while renewing my mind about experiences and past hurts. I am learning how to handle all things in a new, refined way. Equally important, I am training myself to be willing to start over, from the ground up when God says it's time to, yet again.

Therefore, with minds that are alert and fully sober, set your hope on the grace to be brought to you when Jesus Christ is revealed at his coming. As obedient children, do not conform to the evil desires you had when you lived in ignorance. But just as he who called you is holy, so be holy in all you do; for it is written: "Be holy, because I am holy."

-1 Peter 1:13-16

As I wrestle with these daily choices, I am also teaching myself to recognize and fixate on the blessings of God in the small things like those personal messages He sends me through a thought, sermon, or graffiti on a building in passing. I catch myself no longer responding to chaos with matched energy and being able to immediately exercise the word of faith I just finished studying. I've watched God bless me with a teaching job, without knowing that a few months down the line, these students would be a living example of hope for me in a time of despair.

The blessings of God are revealed during the purification process through my nine-year-old little sister when she randomly blurts out Scriptures, verse for verse, with a smile of joy on her face. I see His blessings when my twenty-six-year-old sister texts me how encouraged she is, using "God" in the same sentence, inwardly knowing she has gone through a period of nonbelief. When my mother and I can now sit down and have a vulnerable, safe conversation about past hurts, I know God's grace is a present help.

God's beauty is shown to me in the friends He *did* allow me to keep and be Loved by. These are friends I can receive guidance and wisdom from, friends who embrace all sides of me; those who encourage me not to compromise the real me. God has blessed me with friends who remind me everything's going to be alright even as we continue to fight the dysfunctions of life.

Awe and anguish, simultaneously.

We can't keep everything,
but what God allows us to keep is worth everything.

We are graciously invited to know His Love personally. The cost of this is relinquishing our perspective of Love, releasing our experiences with tainted love and being open to learning Love in a new way, *doing* Love in a new way. A way that costs us our personal preferences because these natural, fleshly desires take us off the deep end. We often reject Love, wisdom, and understanding because we struggle to trust God's goodness over our own. But He is the only good thing this world will ever know. So, we ought to choose life, regardless of what, or *who*, we have to let go of.

Table of Contents

Entry 1

Jhene Aiko
Taught me
To just let the words flow.
It doesn't have to make sense.
It doesn't have to be well put together.
Just write it.
Right it.
Whatever comes
Let it.

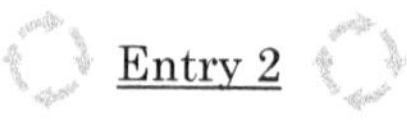

Entry 2

I think it's time.
Time to spread
My wings
& fly.
Share my gift
Of poetry
With the people.
The thoughts
Of this heart
God gave me.
This gift
To glorify Him with.
To liberate His people.

Life is beautiful.
As I lay
In the warm sand
& marvel at the free
Ocean waves.
They come & go
As they please.
Without regard
For who likes them.
Who can handle them.
Who will ride the wave.
Or be overtaken.

Who will curse it
For simply existing
& flowing the way
God ordained it.
I too am like this ocean.
Big & beautiful.
Wide & deep.
Truly immeasurable.
Uncontainable.
Free being
Who God meant
For me to be.

No longer can I wait
To send the next wave
Of purifying water.
Cleansing.
Trying to see if "they"
Can handle me.
No longer can I hold back
My beautifully bold
Wave of depth
Because "they'd" hate
To get washed clean.
This potent saltwater
Is me.
Jesus told me
In Matthew 5:13.

People complain
About the very thing
Jesus told me
Was my identity.
My saltiness
May burn open wounds.
But it also cleans.
It preserves.
It brings back to life
Dying things.
So respectfully
The crashing of my waves
Were never for you
To get to determine
The when.
The why.
The how strong
& how long
She stays.
But if you step
Into my water.
Into my waves.
Guarantee
You will be washed new.
My waves
Tend to wounds.
They aren't here
To overtake you.
They're here to
Heal you.

I'd advise
That you learn
How to ride
& you'll really enjoy
This move.
But if not
That's okay too.
You can curse me.
Stay on the shores.
Stand in the distance
& take your pictures.
As if I'm just
Some showy exhibit.
But regardless
I'm still gonna crash
In & out.
Boldly.
Beautifully.
Freely.
Being exactly
Who God called
Me to be.

This is freedom :)

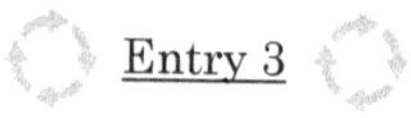

Entry 3

With him
I experienced a hurt
that I had never experienced before.
A hurt that influenced me
to do something that I had not done
in over 2 years
to cope.
A hurt that made me cry myself to sleep
every night.
A hurt that made me feel as if
I was going mentally insane.
A hurt that made me
unable to sleep through the night.
A hurt that made me *hate* the nighttime.
A hurt that made me burst out into tears
in the middle of the day.
A hurt that I felt
within the depths of my being.
A hurt that literally made me sick
to my stomach.
A hurt that made me want to throw up
every time I thought about it.
A hurt that broke me down mentally
emotionally & physically.
A hurt that I honest to God
never imagined recoverable.
A hurt that had satan whispering
lies in my ears
as tears welled up in my eyes.

A hurt that made me feel so alone.
A hurt that made me want to go to work
every day
so that my thoughts couldn't get the chance
to take me out.
A hurt that made me afraid to sleep alone
because I was so tormented in my mind.
A hurt that influenced me
to constantly be on the go
& busy myself
so I wouldn't think about the wound.
A hurt that I clearly remember stating
from the depths of my heart
"I wouldn't wish this upon my worst enemy."
A hurt that tore me down.
A hurt that emptied me.
A hurt that taught me
to never let another guy do this
to me.

A hurt that brought me to my knees.
A hurt that sewed Jesus & I together
for eternity.
A hurt that taught me
to value myself–
one of God's most beautiful creations.

A hurt that saved me.
A hurt that healed me.
He hurt me.
He hurt me in a way that no one
has ever done before.
& he thinks he deserves a second chance
to remain in my domain?
Psh.
Try again.

Even my close friend in whom I trusted, who ate my bread,
has lifted his heel against me.
-Psalm 41:9 ESV

Entry 4

If you try to complete a job
That was not meant for you
You'll see yourself as a failure
& God doesn't want that for you

The things you'll invite into your being
& life
Will become too heavy
A burden to bear
Being that God never even told you
To go there
Removing oneself from the covenant
Of the Lord
Is undoubtedly the worst thing
One can do
It is walking away from safety
Welcoming the invitation
To be screwed...

Well, this is something I wish I always knew.

#woundedbutlearning

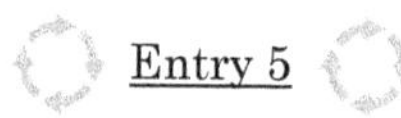

Entry 5

Just because they want you
doesn't mean they deserve you.
& just because they don't deserve you
doesn't mean they're bad people.
They're just not good for you.
They will force you
to compromise yourself
as an individual.

 Entry 6 

Moments...
Last a lifetime.
The memories never go away.
When God says
it's time to move on.
Only options
it seems
are to tuck 'em away.
Or reframe.
I still smile at the good ones.
I'll always cry about the bad ones.
I guess that's just the name of the game.
Years later
or today...

 Entry 7 

Everybody doesn't have a good heart
& everybody's not genuine.
That's just the reality of life.
So you gotta figure out
who you are.
& if that is who you claim you are
then that's who you are to be
regardless of the situation.
You don't pick & choose
when you are your specific race
or gender
or when you are
your parents' biological child.
That is who you are
& who you identify yourself as.
So
be that.

Don't let people influence you to backtrack.
You no longer fit.
You backtracking is like
you trying to wear old clothes
that you no longer fit.
(Picture this: you're uncomfortably busting out of clothes
that once fit your body so snug.)

You're struggling
trying to fit into these clothes
while they're laughing at you.
You're in pain
& they're laughing at you.
You are only hurting yourself by backtracking
because while you're slipping on your pimpin'.
They are making a mockery out of you.
You're doing yourself no justice
by backtracking.

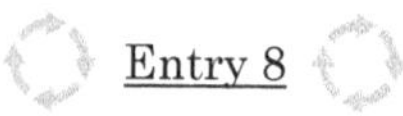

Entry 8

When I see your face
I feel disgust.
Rage floats to the surface next.
& then I begin to reflect
on every encounter we've had
where you've tried to make me
feel less.
"Be small.
Don't speak up for yourself.
Never stand tall for what's right."
That's what I made out of all the
bullshit you'd speak.

I'm small.
But in the Spirit
I'm very tall.
I've learned that
what I have to say matters.
Because of this undying fire
in my belly pit.
If I listen to you
then what happens to me?
Tired of people trying to
make me feel unworthy.
Maybe you're simply projecting
how you feel about yourself
onto me.

& I refuse to accept that.
So satan get back!

Entry 9

I'm the seed.
He's the tree.
& I'm just tryna learn
how to be
who He created me
to be.

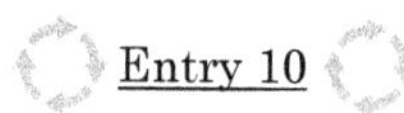

Entry 10

Love & support combined
are two factors that impel *anyone*
to flourish.

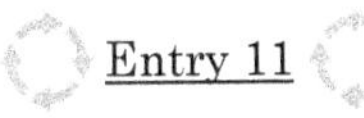

Entry 11

Why would you think
I would switch up
on the only one
that kept it real
from the come up?
Yeah she held it down.
She got one up
on everybody
who's ever tried to come in
& "show up".
She held on to
what was real
even in the times
she couldn't really feel.
Heart was cold
mind was filled
with evil thoughts.
To trade her for you?
Ha!
You must be crazy.
I don't care what battles
we go through
she loves me like
I'm the #1 & only lady.
You
or anyone for that matter
could never equate to who she is today.
The funny part about it is
she hasn't even reached the pinnacle
of her identity.

But yet & still the genuine
caring heart she's got
would still be enough
even if today the growth of that heart
was to stop.
Couldn't see why
they try to diminish
her image
& finish her
when all she ever did
was keep it real.
Even when it would've been easier
to chill.
Catch a thrill.
Pop a pill.
She chose to love herself
when she couldn't love herself.
She chose to love those around her
when they couldn't love her back.
Without a doubt.

I had to write this one for me.
Reflect on who I am
& what they don't see.
Dang right I love me.
& Ima always work
to better myself
because I'm the only one I got
at the end of every day.

I can only be me successfully.

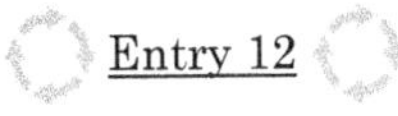

Entry 12

Companionship.
That's what I'm looking for.
Anyone who can
Make me feel
More myself
& less alone.
I need you
To be there for me
After I've had a long day.
Listen to the things
I've been through.
& don't stray away
When I reveal to you
The real me.
But encourage me
To stand in my truth.
& share with me
What you've been through too.

Intimacy.

Entry 13

Is it better to have loved & lost than to have never loved at all?

What are we doing?
I feel like I'm losing.
I feel like I'm wasting my time.
Not really wasting it
because a lesson is always learned.
But I'm tired of getting hurt.
& from here
it can only get worse.
You say you don't know any better.
But I think different.
If you really loved someone
even in times of distress
you wouldn't leave them hanging.
Leave home
just to find yourself banging
another one who you say
is incomparable to your "lady".
It just doesn't make sense to me.
Maybe I'm different.
I've been saying it for years.
I love differently.
Selflessly, patiently, carefully.
I guess I've learned
this is a result
of knowing the Lord Himself.
Who taught me
in 1 Corinthians 13:4-8

Love is patient,
love is kind.
It does not envy,
it does not boast,
it is not proud.
It does not dishonor others,
it is not self-seeking,
it is not easily angered,
it keeps no record of wrongs.
Love does not delight in evil
but rejoices with the truth.
It always protects,
always trusts,
always hopes,
always perseveres.
Love never fails…

Maybe you just haven't learned
how to love yet…

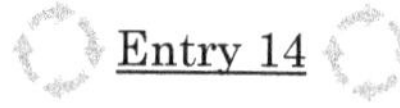

Entry 14

You have to allow people
to go through their process.
If it wasn't for the experience
I wouldn't have the wisdom.
I would just have facts.

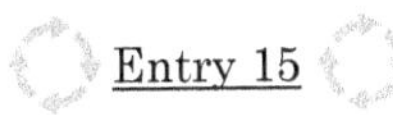

Entry 15

Me: "It's not always about you, ya know?"
Him: "It's not always about you either."
Me: "Yeah, but I have the right to pick & choose & I choose me."

Sometimes to love is to leave.

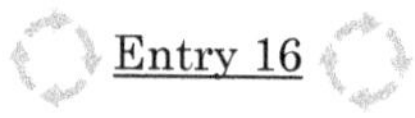

Entry 16

The better
Is the decision
You can have
Peace about.

If you can't choose it
& gain peace
It is not the Love
You claim it to be.

It may have made
Your insides feel fuzzy
& your heart pounce.
His lips may have been
The biggest
Best comfort you've had
In awhile.
But it costed you your peace.

Which confirms the belief
That it had not been
The Love
You claimed it to be.

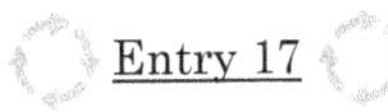

Entry 17

It's so hard to go through breakups
because you become attached to someone
you do not possess the capacity to love
romantically.
Attachment draws you all near
while the inability stands in the way
of cohabitation & continual growth.

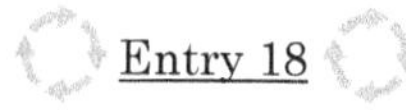

Entry 18

I wanted to be with someone
who looked like him
but acted differently.
What a disgrace I am.
I asked for more
as if *he* isn't enough.
Maybe for me, no.
But he is enough.
& I knew
from the day we met
I was gonna need more.
I should have stopped myself right there.

#SorryForMakingYouFeelIncompetent

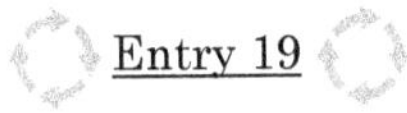

Entry 19

In my view
there's more to life.
In others' view
this *is* life.

Perspective is everything.

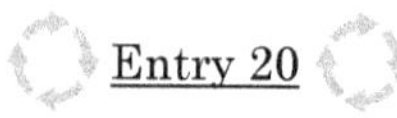

Entry 20

My issue wasn't my relationship with him.
My issue was my relationship with myself.
How I felt about myself.
My insecurities.
My experiences.
My trauma.
My heartbreaks.
& how none of these things
had been dealt with.
Simply suppressed.
Yet still present
because all of these things
impacted my behaviors.
How I moved.
The relationships I engaged in.
Who I entertained.
Because that's what I believed
I deserved.
Maybe he didn't hurt me.
Maybe I was the one
who inflicted my deepest wounds.

#stilllearning

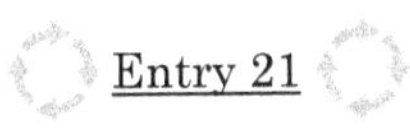

Entry 21

God,
Help me to choose me the way I want somebody else to choose me.
Help me to protect me the way I want somebody else to protect me.
Help me to vouch for me the way I want somebody else to vouch for me.

I have to do the work.
Nobody can do it for me.
But they will do it *with* me if I set the leading example.

Entry 22

The deeper the emotion & experience
Is suppressed
The closer it gets to your core & roots
& from the roots stem all things
So it'll pour into your every move
It'll influence every single thing that you do

Be careful.

Above all else, guard your heart; for everything you do flows from it.
-Proverbs 4:23

Entry 23

We don't want to
experience the pain
that comes with becoming
who God created us to be.
But the ironic part is
we still want to experience pain.
Just pain we're comfortable with.
Drug addictions.
Toxic relationships.
Self-sabotaging behaviors.

New things are scary
because we don't know
what to expect.
Because we are not in control.

This world teaches us
so much about control
& money & power.
& how each
are interconnected.
So that's what we want.
They instill in us
that with these things
come true peace
& success.

Which is a LIE.

& with that truth
I am willing to experience
the pain that comes
with the process of becoming
who God created me to be.

I choose the pain of change
over the pain of staying the same
because I desire *real* peace.
Not temporary tranquility
filled with deceit.
That, to me, is success.

I wanna be free.

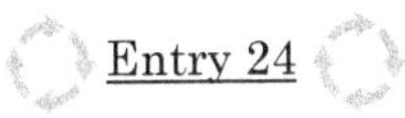

Entry 24

So much responsibility
& a jam-packed daily schedule
Of being pulled in every which way
Causes one to stay out of touch
With herself.

If you are out of touch with yourself
& you allow the world to misuse
& abuse you
Are you really successful?

If you don't know yourself
You don't know the way(s)
In which you can be used
At maximum capacity.
So you'll be used any & everywhere
To fulfill *their* needs.

I lost myself a long time ago
& I've been using all these
Involvements & educational paths
To find myself hopefully
Behind one of these doors.
The more lost I realized I was
The more urgent & frantic
The chase became.
The more elevated
The drain.

I needed a break.

Entry 25

Your commitment is to you
& God only.
If it's not serving God & it's not serving
who God called you to be
it will not prosper.
Understand this.
It will save you a lot of time
& heartache.

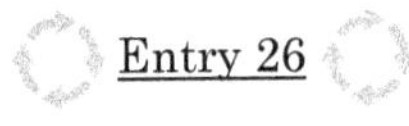

Entry 26

Never more surrounded.
Never more alone.

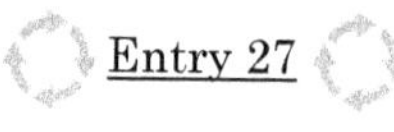

Entry 27

I want what I had
& ain't no way
Ima get that back

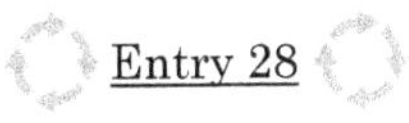

Entry 28

This fleshly body you see
does not always resonate with me.
People assume outer beauty
makes inner beauty
more easily accessible.
Effortless, if you will.
But this body does not determine
my emotions...
my thoughts....
my mistakes...

I have to come to grips
with the fact that
I will always make mistakes
that will indeed make me
feel less than human at times.
& I have to reassure *myself*
as I would another
that I'm still learning
& that it's gonna be alright.

Do you know how hard
that is to do?
To forgive yourself constantly
when you know in your heart
that you *know* better?
But for some odd reason
you can't always seem to apply
that plethora of knowledge
you possess.

It makes one feel shallow.
Incapable.
Stagnant.
Worthless...

But because I know God
I wake up another day
& try again
to learn to love myself
because *He* loves me.
He makes me feel worth something.
He shows me how amazing I can be
& how I'll get through whatever
as long as *we* work together.

Learning to love myself is a task
that I don't know if I'll ever master.
But I have to *learn*
because loving myself first sets the tone
for all else that comes after.
Maybe that's why most people's lives
are in shambles...
If you don't truly love yourself
there's not really much else
you can properly handle.

It's okay though.
The learning opportunity
will always present itself.
You need only allow yourself
to actively engage
in the process.

Forgive yourself.
Every chance you get.
However many times you need.
Look yourself in the mirror
& talk to yourself
as if you were your best friend.
Gently.
Kindly.
& compassionately.
You have to learn
to love yourself
in this experience
on earth.
Love is the very reason
we are here.
So don't spend years here
& miss the purpose.
It's not worth it.

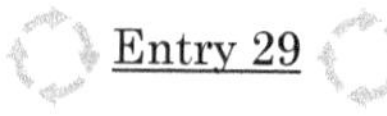

Entry 29

None of this is real.
But it matters.
This experience is similar
to a practice test.
To work out
the spiritual muscles
& gain the skill set.
For the real thing.
Which comes into play
after this life.
Life after.
The afterlife.
The real life.
We must be prepared
to achieve peace
& maintain it.
By any means.
Humbling ourselves.
Learning how to Love.
Letting go of
all that is heavy on us.
We were birthed
to learn, grow & glorify
the One we came from
& the One we will return to.

God's grounds are holy.
He created us in His image.
Which means we are holy, too.
So that's what we must strive for
while here on earth.
Never allowing what's happening around us
to get in or on us
distracting us
from our truest purpose.

#ItMattersWhatYouDo
#ItMattersWhatYouChoose

Therefore, since we are surrounded by such a great cloud of witnesses, let us throw off everything that hinders and the sin that so easily entangles. And let us run with perseverance the race marked out for us, fixing our eyes on Jesus, the pioneer and perfecter of faith. For the joy set before him he endured the cross, scorning its shame, and sat down at the right hand of the throne of God. Consider him who endured such opposition from sinners, so that you will not grow weary and lose heart.

-Hebrews 12:1-3

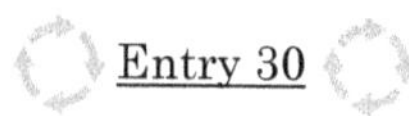

Entry 30

"Is it *Really* Over?"
I feel...
I was with another man last night.
I feel...
As we lay in the bed, he caressed & kissed every inch of my body.
I feel...
I gripped his bulky back muscles & biceps.
My favorite thing to do.
I feel...
He inched from my navel to my neck.
I feel...
Making multiple attempts to kiss my mouth.
But I'd just turn the other way.
I feel...
I forced myself to experience satisfaction but no real spark ignited.
I feel...
As I went through this experience, all I could think of was you.
I feel...
I felt on his body– the muscles, cuts & bulks varied from your own.
I drew back, grew limp.
I feel...
Ashamed & dirty that although we're through,
I gave something to someone else that belongs to you.

All things are wearisome, more than one can say.
The eye never has enough of seeing,
nor the ear its fill of hearing.
-Ecclesiastes 1:8

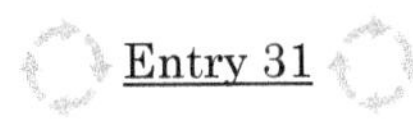

Entry 31

I was needy
& he was present
...
Needless to say
I woke up with regrets

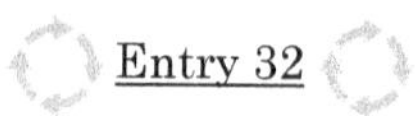

Entry 32

You were never there
when it mattered most.
Graduations & ceremonies
you brought your love tank
on full
& the joy on your face
always made me proud
that I never gave up
when that felt like
the only option.
But the day-to-day struggles
I fought so hard & so long
without you.
There was no room
for me to get tired
because I depended on
my own strength for survival.
Some days my soul feared
not what battle would come
the next day
because I am a fighter.
But the loneliness
that would creep up
& nibble away at
any form of hope
that resided in my heart.

I'd text you good morning
wishing you a peaceful
prosperous day.
Riskfully because yesterday
the energy I sent out
wasn't reciprocated by you.
But I always came back.
I always decided,
"It's a new day.
Let's give it another try."
I didn't hear, "I'm proud of you,"
during the process.
My heart cries for a deep
intimate love with you.

...

Why does it feel like
I am the only one fighting?

#tired

Entry 33

God showed me things.
He plucked me from one place
& gently placed me in another.
For a few reasons:
To intake more rich nutrients.
To allow me to feel a new type of breeze–
one that refreshes my Spirit.
He brought me here to show me Him.

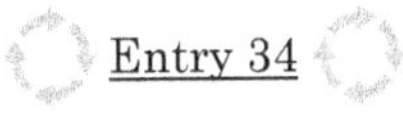

Entry 34

Thank God every day
that He is my Father.
I thank God every single day
that He is my daddy.
When people ask me,
"I am a daddy's girl.
My Father is the true definition
of Love.
Unconditional
beyond any of my shortcomings.
He's been by my side
every step of the way.
It is only because of Him
that I'm as successful
as I am.
His Words relieve my anxiety
& worries.
They bring me peace.
He taught me to cherish myself.
Growing up
He showed me why
I should never settle
for less than the Love
He's given me.
He's held me through
the heartaches & heartbreaks.
He is my rock.
My backbone.
& my strength.
He's my role model.
I love my daddy with everything in me."

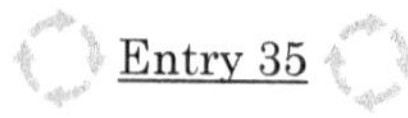

Entry 35

I know it's necessary.
It's inevitable.
It doesn't make it hurt
any less though.
The concepts are logical
& sensible.
But the pain runs deeply
through my veins
during the experience.

This pain I feel
is not my own.
I feel for you.
My heart breaks for you
because you are locked
behind bars.
Caged in,
"To tame the menace to society,"
the system says.
But what they don't understand
is how broken you are.
They didn't take the time
to study your wounds.
Look deeply into them
& identify the root.
There is a little boy
that resides within you.

He yearns for the gentle touch
of a compassionate
attentive mother.
He's learned quick ways
to make money
from the streets
to consider himself a man.
But he's really just a boy.
You're really just a boy.
A broken boy.
& life does everything
in its power
to continue to bruise
& batter you.
My heart breaks for you
because your oldest brother died this morning.
Your right hand.
The one who taught you
every good & bad you know.
The one you fought with
but loved on more.
Loyalty between y'all ran deep.
You two together were a force
to be reckoned with.
Y'all were best friends.
& even though y'all weren't talking
at the moment
they killed your best friend.
My heart breaks for you.
I silently listen to your voice crack
over the phone.

Anger, pain & revenge.
I can feel the energy.
I can hear it in your voice.
My heart breaks for you.
Nobody loves you like a brother does.
Protects you like a brother does.
Cares for you
& wishes so deeply
that you take their advice
rather than their lifestyle actions
as your own.
Because they want you
to be better than them.
I listen to you frantically
question your mom,
"What are we gonna do??!"
You plead & scream,
"Get me out of here!
I don't care what you gotta do.
How much money
you gotta get together.
Get me out of here!
I'm not playing!"
Ugh.
I wish it was all a dream honestly.
I wish I could just wake up
from this cruel experience.
My heart is breaking for you.

Shattering within my body
because you have to walk through this
to get to the other side.
Far too often
the people who should have stayed
left.
They left you
& you had to learn to fend
for yourself.
You have experienced abandonment.
You learned what you could
to get what you needed.
& the system tased you
until you were lifeless.
Locked you up
& left you depleted.
Now
life is happening
all around you.
With or without you.
& although you are watching
from afar
the impact is close
& it undeniably
leaves you scarred...

Entry 36

People make me sad.
Humans make me really sad.
I am never satisfied
with what they seem to give me.
I need more.
I am worth more.
I deserve more.
I feel like I'm in a different place
than everybody else.
They don't see things like I do.
Or feel like I do.
I feel everything
intensely.
When I need someone to run to
where are they?
They don't know how
to be there for me
as I need them to be.
Thinking
"I love yous" suffice
or make up for
the fact that
they don't call
to check up on me.
I mean how do these people
think I make it
day-by-day?

They love the success
of it all
& congratulate me.
But day-to-day
I can't depend on one
for a thing.
I need them to *be* there
for me.
I guess those who show up
for themselves
will show up for you.
Maybe that's where
the disconnect lies...

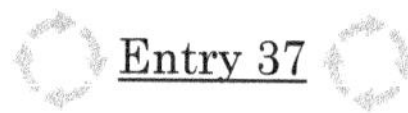

Entry 37

It's like everybody's out there
living their lives.
Numb.
& I feel everything so deeply.
I know what it feels like to be numb
& I refuse to go back.
So I take it one step at a time.
I can't slip.
I won't.

Entry 38

You didn't choose me.
I chose you as my partner
& you didn't choose me.
I have always been picky.
Never *truly* gave a guy my heart.
You were my first boyfriend.
A title that only two can say
they have had in this lifetime
with me.
You wanted me
so I chose you.
I saw your potential
& your heart.
I saw your yearning
for me to be yours
& only yours.
So I chose you.
I disregarded all else.
Everything that came
before me.
Everyone who had you
previously.
Every other person
in my life
that had ever stood
in the way of us
being one.
I chose you.
Wholeheartedly.

I thought that if I gave you
all I had
you would do the same.
I thought you would see
that I was worth more
than the streets.
If I gave it all I had
you would see that
no other female
could compare to me.
None of them could give you
this selfless heart I possess.
This loyalty that built scales
on my eyes
blinding me to every other guy
fighting for a spot in my heart.
It was just us in my eyes.
You & I.
That's all I could see.
That's all I yearned
my life to be.
Just you & me.
I would drop everything for you
to stop & come to your rescue.
I never truly wanted to see you
in pain.
Even when we were at odds
& I allowed disdain to reign.
I thought if I was close to you
during these times
I could heal your heart.

Your body.
Your mind.
Your saddened spirit.
Whether we were on
bad or good terms.
"Love don't change."
If I loved you yesterday
I'll love you more today.
You were my world.

Maybe that's my problem.
I've never really learned
how to *kinda* like
something.
I allow myself to be
consumed by it.
& when you didn't choose me
you broke my heart.
Shattered I mean.
& ever since
I have guarded my heart
from every person who has tried
to get close to me.
Love & intimacy scare me.
Vulnerability terrifies me.
Because I fear pain.
So I busy myself with things
that have a set procedure to them.
Structure.

"Read these pages.
Write this reflection.
Receive this grade."
Nothing is questionable
about that.
It's straightforward
& success is identified
to be easily ensured
as long as I follow
this formula.
But with Love
it's different.
You don't know
that you'll be successful at it.
You put all your eggs
in one basket.
Work overtime.
Get naked & allow your soul
to become one with another...
& you can still fail.
Why would a person want to do that again?

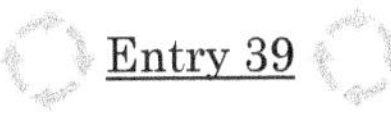

Entry 39

("Write a poem about your First Love")
Fuck him.
He broke the essence
of who I was.
Shredded my esteem.
My trust.
Poked so many holes
in this once strong
heart of mine.
Watched as the kindness
hope & trust gushed
& blamed *me* for the mess
it caused between us.
Infected me with distrust...
I'm never better.
I'm always worse.
Close this heart of mine.
Seal it in the dirt.
I don't want any parts of it.
& I don't need anybody else
selling me
anymore dreams...

I'm out here living emotionless.
& I don't care that they call me a machine.

#inhumane

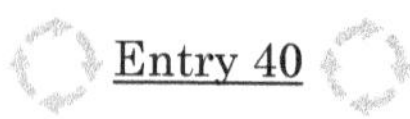

Entry 40

This world is such a dark place man.
& I made a vow to God to be the Light.
Sometimes I reconsider my position
in this mission.
Do you understand what it feels like
being in a pitch-black mansion
with a Light found every 50 feet?
As a Light
I feel lonely
most of the time.
I feel like those like me
are few & far in between.
I typically walk paths alone.
I get it—
to hear God's voice clearly
so I can glorify Him
for my success & achievement.
But it's so painful.
There MUST be another way.
A better way.

I do drugs to cope.
But I don't wanna do that
anymore.
Yes I have slowed down a lot
in terms of quantity.
But I still wanna be able to reflect
& process properly.

I don't wanna be dependent
on something that relieves me
temporarily.
Yet overtime depletes me.
I guess what I'm scared of
is letting go
of this handlebar
without seeing the next one
for me to grab.
Then I get so skeptical
to release my words to others.
I feel like ain't nobody real.
Can't nobody feel
what I feel.
Man all this is temporary.
& I wish the timer
would just beep already!
So we can all disappear
& this cruel simulation could end
gracefully.

#tired

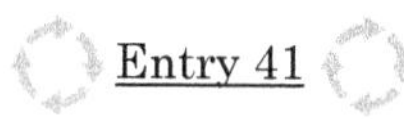

Entry 41

How deep is too deep?
How much is too much?
When do you know if you've gone too far?
You'll only know once you take it there...

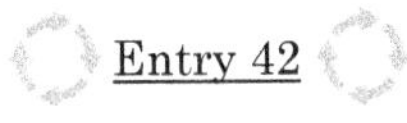

Entry 42

People act like I went through
this whole thing
to stay the same.
I sacrificed my identity.
All that I've known.
Laid down the bad habits
to pick up healthier ones.
I changed everything...
to come back home???

God, why are you sending me back to Egypt?

Entry 43

Loss is inevitable.
My heart cries in agony.
You would think the inevitable
would feel as good as they say
it actually *is*.
If it's happening
& it cannot be stopped
from happening
that essentially implies
its overall goodness
to one's lifelong process.
Yet the inevitability of loss
crucifies me.
It bruises my entire being
swelling my flesh enough to make
my soul ooze out
through the broken cracks.
Slowly, I watch myself
as if an outer body experience.
My body inflamed with tears
of frustration, heartache,
regret, anger.
I watch myself drown...
Do I sit on the sideline & watch?
Willingly or unwillingly?
Able or disabled?

I contemplate getting back in the ring.
If I survive this battle inside here–
The one happening in my mind–
What's the guarantee
of me surviving that battle
out there?
The constant hate & chaos
projected on me from the world.

I wasn't taught how to process
my emotions.
Neither was my mother.
or her mother...
Don't fully know what it feels like
to have grown up with my daddy
by my side during hard times.
Struggled at times having food
& a safe place to stay
growing up.
I fell in love with the other outcasts
that took me in & loved me
when my own family didn't know how.
My family didn't study me enough
to grasp the fact
that it didn't take much
to love me.
Just patience & understanding
as I learned how to love myself.

I've been losing
since before my birth.
So you'd think the inevitability of loss
would have grown on me
by now.
But every time I see an outcast
in the midst of people.
See my brothers locked down in a cell.
Or have to lay down
another one of my black boys.
I relive the inevitability of loss
& I lose a bit of myself each time.

#lost

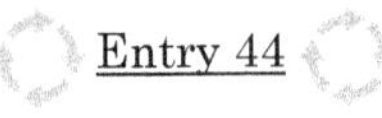

Entry 44

I have just come to the conclusion
that suicide is a common consideration
in human life.
Because of the soul that lies within us
& the fact that we all know
whether consciously,
subconsciously,
or unconsciously
that our lives go beyond
this human experience.
Suicide is a cry for peace.
A soul yearning to be
beyond the chaos
& distress
of this temporary
yet long human experience.
We're all looking for peace.
& from time to time
we indulge in the chaos
because some people
make it seem
like satisfactory happiness...
But I'm starting to learn
they are lying to themselves...
They too are crying out for help.
Just in a different way.
We are all looking for
an escape.

What we really desire deep within
is for our Savior to swoop
into our everyday lives
with His cape.
In our hearts we are all begging
that He comes
& saves the day.
We're all hoping so deeply
that He stays.

All *of creation is groaning.*

We know that the whole creation has been groaning as in the pains of childbirth right up to the present time.
-Romans 8:22

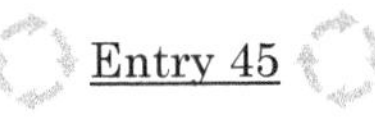

Entry 45

We were two broken people
Trying to love each other
By offering broken pieces
Of ourselves.
The idea of having some part
Of the other was a grand one.
Until you placed it in my hand
& cut me.
I jumped back in astonishment
& anguish
As the blood dripped.
We discussed from afar
& concluded
Maybe if I grabbed it "this" way
It won't cut me.
So we'd come back together
& try again.
Ouch!
The cut grew deeper...
A gash now.
I jumped back
Confused & pained.
It took me longer
To come back together
With you.
Contemplations drew.
Scared I became
Of you.
Of us.

Because every time
We came together
We'd separate more cut up.
How much of it was our fault?
Our parents?
Their parents?
Their parents?
It went beyond us
Because when you came to me
You were broken.
As was I.
& we worked so innocently
Tirelessly
Trying to make all the broken pieces
Fit together perfectly.
I forgive you for cutting me
More than you intended to.
I forgive your mother for the scars
She left on you.
Your father, too.

So now, I would like to
Take things a lot slower.
Allowing the One who made us
To direct us in the placement
Of our energies.

I think we work on fixing ourselves
& leave room for others
To Love & support us
As we work.

Entry 46

I let you in
In hopes that your persistent nature
Persisted once you peeled back the layers
Of my broken heart.
Tarnished from years of anger.
Brokenness & bad behavior.
I made a lot of mistakes
As a youth.
Using things & people to fill the voids.
Whatever would numb my truth.
I let you in
In hopes that I could
Make you better.
Teach you all the lessons
I had to learn on my own.
Because I would never wanna see you
Go down that path
Of life's trials alone.
I'm just praying
You'll make better mistakes than me.
& the closer you get to me
The more I begin to see
That I just wanna give you
All of me.
The wisdom.
My pain.
My naked soul.

But the closer you get
The farther I draw.
Because there's a part of me
That runs away from my feelings.
Vulnerability & all.
I don't know if I'm making any sense
Right now.
Because my thoughts are
Contradicting themselves.
I'm so desperate for Love
Stability & support.
On the other hand
I'm just waiting for the moment
You'll mess everything up.
Cause I've been down this road before.
To tell you the truth
I was conceived in Heartbreak Hotel.
I was born into this.
It's all I've ever known.

Looking to feel something.
Engaging in bad behavior.
It ain't like I don't know no better.
& I promise I ain't tryna live
Like this forever.

I wanna let down my guard
& let my man hold the reins.
I just have this mind-eating fear
That he's not gonna be able to steer...

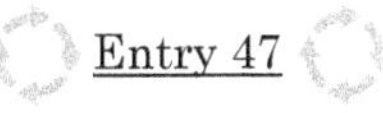

Entry 47

A 2-year situationship
because of my outright fear
of committing myself
to yet another romantic partner.
"I already know how this is gonna end,"
I'd assure myself.
"So let's just be friends."
You'd give anything
to be in my presence.
& when my days
weren't going good
I took advantage.
I'd call you to hang out
& take my mind off of my stress.
By watching you
as you watched me.
I swear I could hear you thinking,
"My beautiful mess."
You made me feel pretty.
Valuable.
& worthy of Love.
Because no matter how many times
I pushed you away
you wouldn't budge.
I thought, "Wow.
Maybe he is the one."
You accepted me
& yearned to build
an everlasting relationship.

But the reality is
during these 23 months together
we barely scratched the surface
of each other's identity
outside of the ideal.
We never truly got to know
what was real.
I'm still figuring out
so much about me.
& I know you're on the same journey.
I recently learned how broken
my heart really is.
Because of my experiences
as a little kid.
& I need you to know
this is a problem you can't fix.
Did you know that
I physically could not
sit in a room alone?
In silence.
& allow my thoughts to roam
up until a few months ago?
There are these voices
inside my head
that bruise & batter me
constantly.

Imagine coming home to me
& all you see is me beat up.
Weak.
& beginning to bleed.
From my wrists.
& my eyes.
But most importantly from my heart.

Could you really understand?
Would you really still want me then?
What could you say to get me to believe
in God's plan again?

Entry 48

Sometimes I get so sad
It scares me.
Because I find myself itching
To be the old me.
Going back to who & what
Broke me.
So desperately hoping
That it'll distract me.
From the challenging experience
Of facing the new me.
Developing these new habits
That I know will sustain me.
It's quite conflicting isn't it?
That I can't seem to totally
Embrace what's best for me.
It brings me great despondency
To sit & realize
How much
I don't fully Love me...

Entry 49

You're a drug to me.
Depleting me of my identity.
I find myself looking like
Sounding like
Thinking like
You.
You diminished my voice
& our dwelling became
A very dark place.
I didn't know who I was
Outside of you
& prayed to God
I wouldn't have to find out.
I knew you weren't any good
For me.
Neither I for you.
& yet here we were.
Co-existing.
Barely.
You made me feel so alive
When we were together.
The beginning was the best.
Electrifying.
Bubbly.
Soothing.

But as soon as I came down
From the high of your love
So did my soul.
The fall felt terrifyingly never-ending.
Maybe that part was my fault.
Because I never wanted us to end.
I am so tired of this cycle
Of love & loss.
I wanted to hold on
To this catch forever.
Even if you drowned me.
How much more enticing was that
Than standing onshore
Watching life happen?

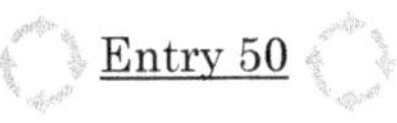

Entry 50

The more I shed light
On my emotions
Connected to situations
They only become intensified.
So at the start
Of this reflective experience
I felt sadness.
But by the end
I've reached such a deep
Dark level
Of self-loathing
& boiling anger
Toward every person
That penetrated this fragile heart
Of mine.
Sorrow is the feeling
I feel
When I think about the people
I've hurt.
The people who've hurt me.
This world is a gloomy place.
Heartbreak is inevitable.
I'm angry that ***I*** have to
Do the healing work
After what *they* did to *me.*

This urges me to never let another in
To my tender heart.
Because all who enter
Intentionally rummage.
Looking for what they can take.
Turn.
Leave.
& act as if it was *I*
Who made the mistake
Of inflicting pain.
Once I check them
Or cut them out of the frame.
As if *I* hurt *them.*
When I poured everything I had!
Even took some of
My mother's belongings
& offered those too.
Why wasn't I enough?
That seems to be
The most prominent question.
Since a girl really.
Why wasn't I enough?

I will never *ever*
Bring a child into this world.
This demeaning dark experience.
With all this pain in my body.
Emotional baggage.
That is one of the most cruel choices.
Allowing my baby to learn trauma
First-hand
From mama.
Being formed
Molded & housed
Where the lack of serotonin
& dopamine
Inevitably causes my baby
To inherit deep sadness
As his or her own.
No
I will never.

 Entry 51 

Brokenhearted little girl
My heart aches for you.
Trying to find your way
In this big world maze.
No one stayed in place
To teach you the way.
In your unknowingness
You actively engaged
In relationships with people
Who manipulated you.
Abused your innocent heart.
Devalued you.
& sent you down a path
Of further confusion & self-hatred.
In your frustrations
You stripped yourself
Of your very power–
The access to a sound, sober mind
By smoking until you were physically stuck
Trying to slow your world's revolve down.
The tears that filled your eyes at night
Truly distorted the image of you.
"I see you," I'd speak.
"Even if they don't."
But your mind's cries have always been louder.
You never wanted to hurt anyone
So I'd watch you hurt yourself instead.
Because pain was an ever-present experience for you
So what did it matter, who it came through?

Brokenhearted little girl
My heart aches for you.
No one really knows what you've been through.
Oftentimes, not even you.
"Suppress, don't address,"
are the words you speak to yourself.
Until you're on your third or fourth drink
& every emotion begins pouring out
Just as fast as your poured up
To mentally "get out".
Brokenhearted little girl
My heart aches for you.
Mommy & daddy were too busy
In their own mess
That they couldn't see the mess
They bore you into.
I know, baby love.
I know.
They didn't see you.
But I do.
I always have.
As your heart broke
From the weight of expectations placed
Yet no real guidance gave...
That shattered heart began to cut
Everything within you.
Internal organs were penetrated
& you started to die on the inside.

Brokenhearted little girl
My heart aches for you.
Because even when the cuts became external
Still, mommy & daddy were too busy to see.
All they see is that their little girl is unhappy.
But they'd never give you the chance to speak.
Because that means coming face-to-face with their truth.
Truly evaluating the life that they gave you.
I know you wanna ask him,
"Why didn't you wanna be my daddy?
You only came around when I was in trouble.
Why didn't you just stay?
I promise I would've stayed out of trouble."
Let mommy know you forgive her
For putting more on you
Than you could bear.
Because her other children's fathers
Were never there.
Brokenhearted little girl
My heart aches for you.
Because you had to fight for yourself
Since day one.
Fight to survive
While *trying* to thrive.
See, no one knows the real thoughts
You have about yourself.
Unworthy of Love.
Not good enough.
Not mentally strong enough.
Unsure of your existence.
Insecure of your capabilities.

Yet here you are.
Still.
Fighting to survive.
Brokenhearted little girl
My heart aches for you.
Because you don't see yourself
As I see you.
Not everybody can put on your shoes
& successfully make it through
All the hoops.
You taught yourself
Discipline, focus,
Self-motivation, *and* determination.
& you wear it damn good!
Or what about the ways
You desperately seek
To be healed
& hold yourself accountable
For your healing.
That's admirable.
You are honorable.
You are noble.
You are strong & wise.
Brokenhearted little girl
My heart aches for you.
& I pray that God sees you through
As you come to understand & know
The real you.

When my father and my mother forsake me,
Then the LORD will take care of me.
-Psalm 27:10 NKJV

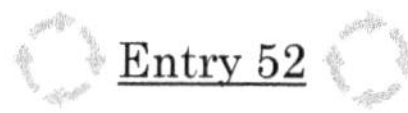

Entry 52

Writing allows your experiences
to never die.
That's the scary part about it.

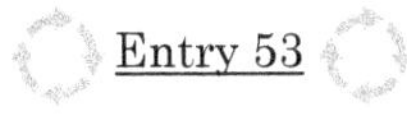

Entry 53

I'm sorry God
that I walked away from us.
Thinking I could choose
a better way.
I know I don't read Your Word
every day.
But every day.
Every single day.
Every *single* day
I try to be the best me.
Standing for unity
& peace.
For You.
For me.

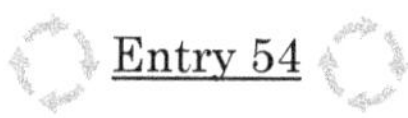

Entry 54

Keep me sweet & tender
Toward You.
Continue to light this fire
Of overwhelming desire
To please You.
Above all else...

 Entry 55 

"Trust Issues"
I know who You are.
Although I haven't always.
They struggle to see Your face.
The red fury
combined with
the clouded tears
in their eyes
warp the image of You.
This world has destroyed
the very innocence
of us all.
"Trust me," it says.
As it lures us in
with sole intentions
of taking advantage.
Our young, pure hearts
followed what
we thought was right.
Who we thought
would protect us.
Just for it to strip us.
Piece by piece.
With a smile on its face.
Hearts collapsed.
Innocence & purity leaked slow.
That's when the fight for survival began.
Because this wasn't the last time
we were taken advantage of.

That was just the beginning
of the ongoing cycle
of destruction & desolation.
Affliction & anger.
The initiation of a life of abuse.
& then You come along
trying to provide a new storyline
ending with, "Trust me."
I got trust issues man.

If You are
who You say You are
then You must have seen it all.
All that I've endured.
From the fake family
to the back-stabbing friends
& the many men
who toyed with the delicacy of
my feminine energy.
Y'all got one thing in common–
wanting my trust.
But what makes *You* so different?
I told You.
I got trust issues man.

"Watch me," He replied.
So I did.
Very intently.
For many years.
He did what He said He would.

He was a God
of peace, love & a sound mind.
Some days I found myself brokenhearted
after flirting with the familiar life of abuse.
But He stayed put.
He never moved.
He was faithful to me.
Even when I couldn't be faithful
to myself.
Every time my heart broke
he brought me a bundle of 9 flowers.
Each possessing its own significance–
Love, joy, peace,
patience, kindness, goodness,
faithfulness, gentleness & self-control.
Overtime, my trust issues dissipate
thanks to Him.
I have finally met someone trustworthy.
Honest.
Genuine.
The others have yet to hear Your voice.
Therefore they can't see Your face.
They are bruised, bashed,
& still afraid.
Every ounce of them cries.
Some loudly.
Some silently.
I pray that they let You in
so they will no longer have
trust issues.

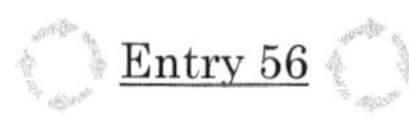

Entry 56

Even when I thought
I lost it all...
Still remaining
Was His goodness & mercy.
Regenerating glory.

(Thanks Mrs. Erica)

Surely goodness and mercy shall follow me all the days of my life and I will dwell in the house of the Lord for ever.
-Psalm 23:6 KJV

 Entry 57 

I'm always looking to produce.
Looking to juice myself
of my very existence
essentially.
Because I'm making time for everyone
& everything else.
Except me.
What about me?
Even in my times of sleep.
Prior to
all I do is think.
Think of who I am.
For which causes I stand.
What's in my hands.
Things that I'm willing to share
with the mass of man.
I believe my life has been created
for that very reason–
to produce for the masses.
So while I'm here
laying my head to sleep
all I can do is think
about who & how I will impact.

What do I have to learn?
Who do I have to become
so that those around me
will be healed
through me?

-living sacrifice

Entry 58

Why do you care
what others think of you?
If you know what's true
what does it matter
who's thoughts are parallel to you?
Most don't love themselves enough
to spend time getting to know the truth.
Within themselves.
Within the world.
& the truth of those
they expose
themselves to.
So again I ask you
what does it matter
what others think of you?

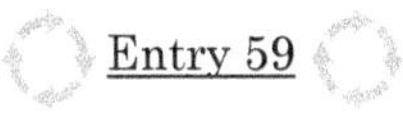

Entry 59

As I sit here
In a dark room.
Overwhelmed with life.
Dissatisfied with my placement.
My choices.
My surroundings.
My environment.
... my fate.
It hits me.
I've reached rock bottom again.
I've actively participated
In the anchoring of my soul
To the bottom of the ocean
Of emotions...
I've invited heavy things
& people
Into my entire being.
I just wanna get away.
From here.
This city.
This family.
This body.
These emotions.

Stop the internal motion.

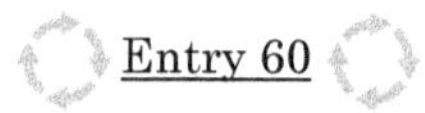

Entry 60

He's just like
The fucking rest
Cause he let
His flesh
Get the best

Finesse.
Caress.
Undress.
Oppress.
Obsess.
Stress.
Depress.
Address.
Process.
Digest.
Digress.

Sick of this mess

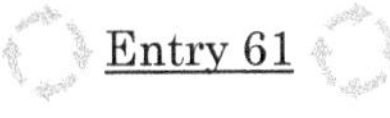

Entry 61

We love toxic relationships
Twonnie can you help me to understand
cause you've made it to the Promise Land

 Entry 62

Every time I open my heart
it gets broken.
& You tell me
not to close it.
It's the most frustrating thing.
I'm so fearful
of opening my heart
for You
& to You
because then comes confronting
& making amends
with every person
who has broken me.
& I can't do that right now
because I don't believe
in my heart
they deserve it.
I don't wanna get
my heart broken anymore.
I won't.
It fucks up my trust.
With people.
With myself.
My self-esteem.
My hope.
I become unhopeful.
& people become distasteful.
& I'd rather be by myself
because I self-destruct occasionally
just fine.

I'll never be ok.

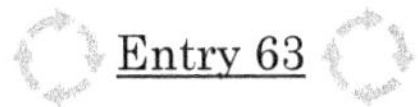

Entry 63

Do I not hate those who hate you, LORD,
and abhor those who are in rebellion against you?
I have nothing but hatred for them;
I count them my enemies.
-Psalm 139:21-22

....

I hate that I'm supposed to hate him.
I hate that he broke my heart.
I hate that he set it up to where I now have to hate him.
I hate that I can't hate him.
I hate that I still love him.
I hate that I love him more than I love me.
I hate that I don't know how to hate him.
Even though he broke me
I'm still willing to learn how to love him
with all the little broken pieces of me.

I hate discord & division.
Why did you have to pick that side?

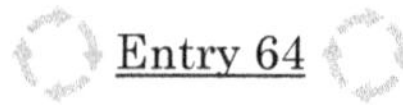

Entry 64

I feel defeated
to the utmost degree.
I don't care
about the decisions of others.
How they negatively affect themselves
or those around them.
I don't care to intervene.
I feel anger.
I feel hurt.
I feel constant heartbreak.
Every mistake I've made.
Every person who's crossed me.
I think about these things
far too often.
I want them to feel my pain.
I don't care what happens after.
I refuse to consider consequences.

I'm not thinking about preparation
for work tomorrow.
I have to advocate for those kids.
I am their voice
while people believe they are too small
to have one.
That's all I really care about in this world
is the kids.
I hate it here.
I hate this world.
I hate this place.

I don't wanna be here anymore.
I've lost hope for myself.
How can I think about my future
when I can't get through my present?
People hurt me.
I hurt myself.
It's inevitable.
It was written
before the beginning of all this.
So tell me
what's the point
of me fighting?
When all else is fighting against me.
Including me.
I'm tired of this cycle–
falling off to pick myself back up.
On a good streak.
Just to get hurt.
& again
fall off.
I can just stay off
& hopefully die.
Get away from all this.

They took my cousin!
I wanna be with him.
Maybe I don't deserve paradise
but
I wanna be anywhere
but here.

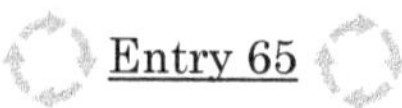

Entry 65

What if my life is never worth anything to me?
I'm always doing it for someone else.
Why can't I get it right for me?
You don't know these screwed up thoughts
I have about myself naturally.
So, for you to put me down hurts.
It makes me feel worse.
Nobody can treat me worse than myself.
I always wish somebody can help teach me
how to treat myself.
But they come in & break me.
Effortlessly.
Regretlessly.
I just wanna be to myself
because I can do all that soul-cutting
all by myself.
So thanks a lot
but no thanks.

I'm tired of this heartbreak.

 Entry 66 

When you break my heart
you break my trust
& dismantle my hope.
Not only for you
but for myself too.
& for all those
who follow
after you.

I'd rather be alone.

 Entry 67 

I write best
when I'm the most suicidal.
It's like that's when
it's the realest.
The most raw.
Truly relatable
because of the fall...
My Spirit cries
as my soul breaks.
In so many places
I can't seem to take.
I feel heavy.
I feel drowned.
I don't even experience
this life of bliss
everyone thinks
for which I've earned
the crown.
I go inward.
All is black.
It's like logically
everything is out of whack.
I feel like everyone is against me.
But more than them
is me.
I'm my worst enemy.
I hate myself with everything in me.
Not like there's much left in me
once I get to this point
typically.

But it frightens me.

Yet at the same time
it soothes me.

The fact that I could
let go of everything
in that very moment
& feel no care for it
is just as liberating
as it is scary.
I guess the worst part of it all
is coming face-to-face
with the fact that
I say I love this God.
Yet can possess
such a great capacity
of hate.
Disgust.
Distrust.
& unforgiveness
for the very thing *He* created
to carry my soul
& His Spirit
in.

I think that's what hurts the most.

I pray that one day
I can forgive myself
for both the mistakes
& the self-hate.

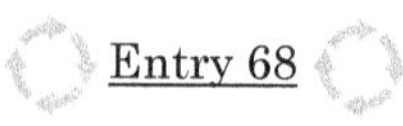

Entry 68

Because I always
make it happen
they thought I'd be okay.
& they'd tend to the ones
who seemed more needy.
But no one knew
what I went through
in the dead of the night
for years.
Mentally imprisoned.
Suicidal.
Internal conflict constantly.
Trying to get away from people
who didn't respect my boundaries
or honor the authentic me
I was working so tirelessly to be.
Nobody to count on but me
& G-O-D.
Because they couldn't see
the scars they left on my heart
& those left on my arms
by me.
Just trying to be free.
Mentally.
Emotionally.
Spiritually.

#lonely

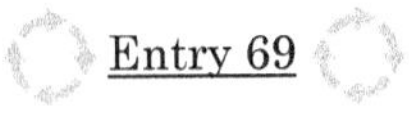

Entry 69

The story we have to tell
will keep us out of hell.
Transparency will break
the generational curses.

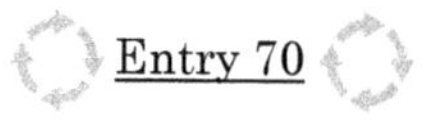

Entry 70

True Love is a daily work.

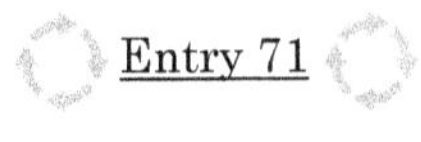

Entry 71

Reading just takes me
to a whole new reality.

-escapism

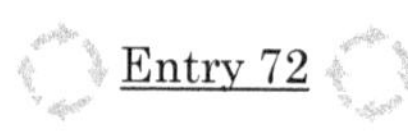

Entry 72

How many people
do we have to lose
before we get it right?

Tired of these streets
& the gun violence.

Dying Internally.

I just wanna be free from depression & defeat.

God, [when] will I ever be free?

Entry 73

These kids need all of me
but I don't even have
all of me to give...

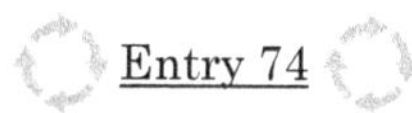

Entry 74

The amount of sorrow we face
leads you to believe
there's no better tomorrows
we'll ever have to chase.

Death is such a heavy experience.
It makes me envy the dead.
Those who don't have to go through
the sorrow of the loss
of a loved one.
While simultaneously
losing oneself.

#LosingMe

 Entry 75 

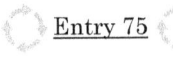

Wasn't no hatred
in my heart
'til that happened
that shit changed me

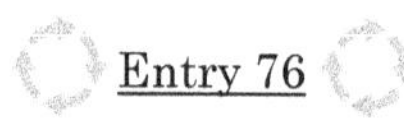

Entry 76

I ain't got no faith
Just a pretty face

Desperately looking for an escape
I can't wear this cape
Can't run this race
I'm so out of shape

#HealTheHood

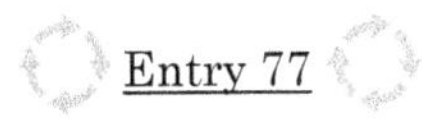

Entry 77

I'm everybody's dream girl
but I'm not even the love
of my own life

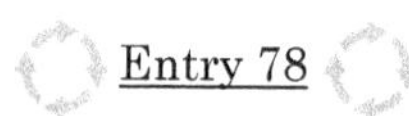

Entry 78

People can want y'all
to be together all day
every day
but if y'all are not
compatible & willing
it won't work.

I don't need the world's advice on my love life.

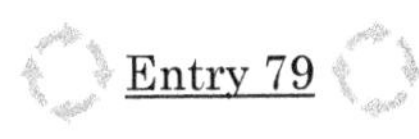

Entry 79

He was willingly
My escapism

 Entry 80 

If you're coming with me
come on.
Let's go.
All that other shit
is gonna have to go.
The jealousy.
Disloyalty.
Unforgiveness.
& no trust.
You gonna have
to be honest.
Let's talk about it.
Then release.
See cause where I'm going
we ain't got time to be distracted.
I'm already training daily
to fight the outside world–
a world full of lies.
Neglect.
No love.
No self-respect.
I don't need any of that
coming from my inner circle.
We supposed to be building
each other up
cause we know
when we go out into the world
we gots to hustle.

Even before we get out there
it's a struggle.
Mentally, internally
I'm fighting me.
The old me fighting
so ruthlessly.
Relentlessly.
To simply be.
She's trying to exist
in a place
where truthfully speaking
there is no longer
any room for her.
So I'm battling the world.
Sometimes me.
& then I gotta worry about you too?
Nah.
That's not what we about to do.
That's not how it's finna be.
I admit my wrongs.
I'm working every day
to make it right.
But one thing I am learning
is that I won't spend my life
tryna prove to you people
my worth.
I'm still tryna prove it
to myself.

The more I look back
on my life...
Tuh, my plight!
I realize how much of a dope individual
I really am.
No matter how much
my heart has been damaged.
Or how deep I have been cut.
Carving some of my own wounds.
I still fight day in & day out
to love again.
To commit to the evolution of me.
To release the negativity.
Cut off certain parts of me.
I'm constantly recreating my identity.
Trying to figure out
which works best for me.
I don't have time
to be at war
with you too.
You're supposed to be
the one who loves me
through every moment
of self-hate I experience.
Every bit of self-doubt.

When I can't even stomach the fact
that I've made yet another mistake.
Entertaining a lower frequency
of myself.
You're supposed to be there!
Not elsewhere.
You shouldn't be
trying to make this shit harder
for me.
You *know* me!
You know what I've been through.
What I constantly tread through.
My dreary past
that lingers over me
like a dark cloud.
My heavy future
that's forever
spitting out commands
at me.
There's so much responsibility.
Behind me.
In front of me.
All around me.
& I'm not saying
I can't take it.

What I'm saying is
you're supposed to be
rooting for me...
But if not
then fuck it.
Because Ima always bounce back
from any change.
All this time around me
& you still ain't recognize my name?
This is Imani
aka Faith.
Forever believing in what I can't see.
Which is the best version of me.
But Ima get there eventually.
Regardless of who supports me.
At the end of the day I know for a fact
God got me.
& that's really the only reason
I am who I am.
Where I am.
Because even when I couldn't hold on
He kept holding me❤

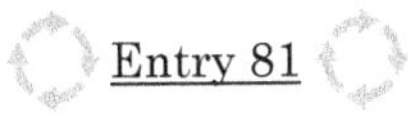

Entry 81

I close my eyes
To go to sleep
Because this pain–
It's too much to keep.
When I sleep
I don't feel a thing.
Don't even dream.

I'm at peace.

Then for whatever reason
When the person I'm in bed with
Gets up to leave
I wake up
& realize
Nothing has changed
Around me.

:(

I still feel this pain.
I wish I could drink
So I could be numb.
But I promised God
I wouldn't drink anymore.
I made a promise to Him
The last time He rescued me
From the grips of that bottle.

The way it squeezed
The life out of me.
I couldn't breathe.
Couldn't even help myself
Get free.
Being drunk causes me
To become vulnerable.
(I never want just one)
Unaware of my surroundings.
Pouring out with emotions.
Focused on the current reality.
This present hell
That I experience.
Unable to create
My healed future
Because all I can see & feel
Is the now.
What's real.

I'm consumed.
Beyond the drink.
It taints everything
I think.

I can't fix my eyes on Jesus.
All my energy is fixed
On my heart.

I watch it explode violently
Into a million little pieces
& hope slips.
It's becoming more apparent.
More prominent a thought.
That there is not a chance
My heart can be rightfully
Put back together again.

I feel so sad
That I had to lose y'all
To gun violence.
People don't even value
The human life.
Right about now
I can relate.
I don't value my life in totality either.

I know I have power.
But I also know I have pain.
& if I could let it all go
To get rid of
This heart-wrenching hurt
I feel.
I swear I would.

But my community needs me.
To be an answer.
I got family.
Siblings.
Friends.
Kids.
They would be distraught if I go.
I wouldn't want them to feel this pain
That I'm feeling.

I will bear the pain
So they don't have to.

Entry 82

Sometimes I wish I was dead.
To me
Death represents end.
End to the pain & suffering
We experience on earth.
End to the exposure
To ungodly things.
End to the temptation
To retaliate evilly.
I just want peace of mind
& I don't wanna work for it.
I don't wanna maintain it.
I just wanna get it.

I'm so tired of working
To maintain happiness.
Tired of it being stolen right through
The cracks of my fingers
Every time I get a grip on it...

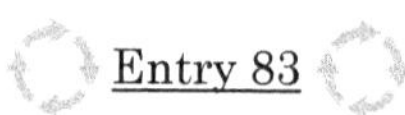

Entry 83

I pray
that I don't get
down on myself
for the mistakes
but that I also
don't become content
with the choices.

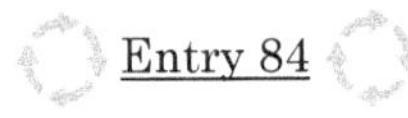

Entry 84

The issue is
we use it to make
the pain go away
but if you're a believer
you know
only God can heal your pain.
Like *truly* heal you.
The other stuff
will never truly heal
or satisfy you.
Just numb you
for the moment.

#searchingforhealing

 Entry 85 

What do you do
when you're all alone
& can't stand the sound
of your own thoughts?
Some days I'm terrified
to be by myself
because I think I won't survive.
So I entertain myself
with TV.
Social media.
People even.
I sleep next to them for comfort.
I don't know how
but having a physical body
next to me
sometimes calms the voices down.
Other times
it intensifies them.
Until I just fall asleep.

Sleep is peace.
Sleep is the closest I get
to making the voices stop.
But sometimes
I have dreams.
Dreams about my thoughts.
The other night
I had a dream
about the death
of a loved one.

It's like I can't get away
from this pain.
Even when
I am intentionally seeking
the good.
Pain comes to visit again.
Perpetually trying to seep
into my bloodstream
& become a part of me.
Sometimes
I have no fight left in me.
So I succumb
& become one
with the pain.
& I feel so drained.
Before you know it
I've literally gone insane.
Wanting to end it all.
No one knows
what goes on in my brain.
It's like a constant war zone.
That I don't think
I'll ever fully win...
& with that thought
I simply give in again
& become one
with the pain.

I need saving.

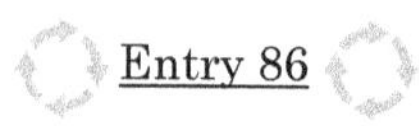

Entry 86

How are *you*
gonna tell me *anything*
about relationships
when you cheat
on your significant other
every chance you get
& vise versa?
Fuck outta here...
What happened to integrity?
What are you trying to
teach me?
I refuse to eat what you feed!
If I continue to
it'll be the death of me...

Do not be deceived,...whatever a man sows,
that he will also reap.
-Galatians 6:7 NKJV

Just do it differently.
So that you are able
to receive
what you really wish
to receive.
Which is *real* Love
& reciprocity...

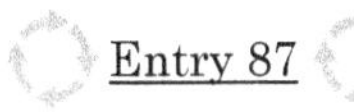

Entry 87

As I drive around
the city of Miami
I reminisce
on the memories I made
with him & his family.
& every car I see
driving closest to me
leads me to believe
it's him in there
staring back at me.
But I know it's not meant to be...
So why do I miss you?
Why does the human mind trick me?
I wish there was something
I could use to numb me
& freeze this feeling
until it's so cold
& small enough
to break apart within me.
Decaying slowly.
But God tells me
I'm meant to feel everything
that I feel.
So what do I do with what I feel?
Maybe I should ask Him–
the Father.

Stop looking to these men to fix me
& start letting in
the Father.
When they said,
"Let him use you,"
maybe they were talking about
the Father...

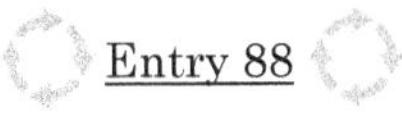

Entry 88

He did some
hurtful things
to me.
He hurt me.
& it hurts me
that it hurts still...
When he hurt me
that was my cue
to deal with him
in a different manner

— *boundaries.*

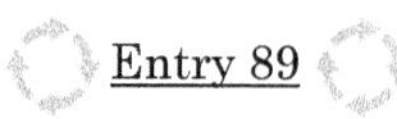

Entry 89

I wish he would make it right.
I wish he could heal
what *he* broke in me...
but I know he can't.
I've been here
too many times before.

 Entry 90 

Baby face.
My purest state.
Been learning to Love
parts of me
I've told myself
over the years
is hard to take.
When it's all said & done
all I got is this one—
mind, body, soul, & Spirit.
So the best care
I gotta take♡

— *self-love*

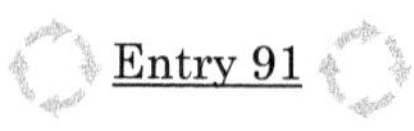

Entry 91

I'm grateful
that God looked
beyond my flaws
& saw my needs

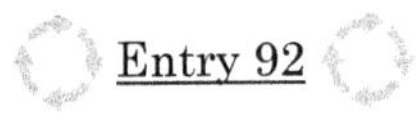

Entry 92

I miss it
But it was loveless

Entry 93

You will always be
a part of the story
of me...

Entry 94

It's actually when
we don't feel anything
that something is known
to be wrong.

It's okay to feel.
It's inhuman not to.

What intimate relationship
do you know of
that's convenient?

Entry 96

Highs & lows...
Sometimes in the moment
We never really know
What comes next–
Failure or success?
Heartbrokenness
Or bliss?
But as I sit back
& look at my life
I realize
Neither one is
"Just right."
We need both
To understand & grow.
The highs keep us encouraged.
Hopeful, motivated.
The lows allow us to
Stay in touch with reality.
Sometimes showing us
Who & where
We don't wanna be.
& why we must keep fighting
To be holy.

Life can be ugly.
Life does possess beauty.
Death hurts.
Death hurts so bad
I don't even possess
The vocabulary to truly express
The sorrow I feel
When it comes to death.
My hope is demolished.
My vision blurred.
Identity evaporates
& I'm lost for words.
It's like I shrink
Into nothingness
& don't care to be much more.

& then Spirit cries out.
Begging to be nurtured.
Screaming for an ounce
Of water.
Holy water.
The internal conflict kills me.
So I give in
& begin to look for God again.

I find Him in the simplest of things.
Like sunsets, children, laughter.
Kind words & Loving gestures.
He reminds me
That it's the little things
That really matter the most.
What would life be
Without the soothing
Ocean waters?
Big beautiful mountains?
Cute complimentary notes?
& smiling strangers on the street?
Although situations & circumstances
Do shift throughout life
This is where our focus must be.
This is how we truly
Gain peace.

Thank You God.

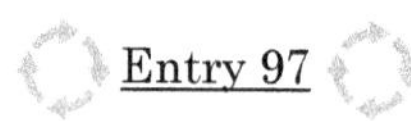

Entry 97

It wasn't in vain
& it wasn't just for the pain

– pain to purpose

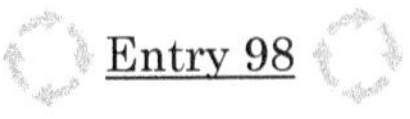

Entry 98

This girl
Will always be
Your little girl.
Daddy's girl.
To her
You mean the world.
She looked.
She loved.
She lost
While she was outside
In the world.
Brokenhearted
She trotted
Back home
To You.
No one even knew
What she had put herself through.
I guess the Love
Of You
Wasn't always known
& understood
By her premature mind.
& so she tried
To find
Things & people
To stop the tears
That flowed
From out of
Her eyes.

She used the drugs
To numb her entire being–
Body & soul.
Hoping that she wouldn't
Have to feel anything
Anymore...
The boys were supposed to
Fill the voids
Once she let them inside her.
But once penetrated
It was as if
They pumped more sadness
Shame
& guilt
Through her body
With every stroke.
A blow
To her self-confidence.
A blow
To her self-image.
A blow
To her self-worth...
& more suicidal
She became.

But You oh God
You brought sunshine
Again.
You brought hope.
My favoritest friend.
You cleansed me
From the shame
Of my youth.
(Isaiah 54:4)
You healed me
By helping me confront
The truth.
The truth is I'm made right
In Your sight.
The truth is Jesus died
So I could be justified.
The truth is
You value me.
& I don't need to be
Out in these streets
On those drugs
Or with those guys
In order to be loved.
The truth is
You fill every void.
You have taught me
The goodness of
Being alive.

You've given me purpose
& direction.
Thank You for being here
With me through every season
Of becoming my truest self.
Thank You for being my fix
When I couldn't depend
On anyone else.

You restore me.

For I will restore health to you, and your wounds I will heal,
declares the LORD, because they have called you an outcast
'It is Zion, for whom no one cares!'
-Jeremiah 30:17 ESV

Entry 99

The start of something new.
Who would've thought?
But God knew.
Your plan could never
Be stopped.
You brought us together
For a time as this.
For true healing.
Love, happiness
& bliss.
Each individual
With a story
Of brokenness.
Insecurity.
& multiple false identities.
Who would've thought
We'd make it
To the Promise Land
Before our ascending transition?
When we gave You
The broken pieces
You birthed magic
In each of us.
Thank You Father
For allowing us to
Experience each other.

Thank You for Jesus' blood.
Allowing it to cover
Every mistake.
Each shortcoming
& intentional choice
That separated us from You.
Thank You for bringing all
The parts of You
Back together.
As we sit in this house
To worship You.
Truly in this room
There's only You.
Thank You for Your Love
As it pulls us
From out the dark places
Back into Light.
Thank You for teaching us
That it is only *Your* strength
That will win every fight.
You have brought us
Into a world of chaos
& yet have called us
To be peace.
Thank You for equipping us
To navigate this journey.

With the fruits of Your Spirit
& my beautiful homies :)
God You are Love
& I am forever grateful
For the extensions of You
You've chosen to share.
Continue to use us
To peel back each other's layers
Until all is pure.

Amen.

Let us hold tightly without wavering to the hope we affirm, for God can be trusted to keep his promise. Let us think of ways to motivate one another to acts of love and good works. And let us not neglect our meeting together, as some people do, but encourage one another, especially now that the day of his return is drawing near.

-Hebrews 10:23-25 NLT

Entry 100

The only way to survive
Is to read the book of Life
With your eyes
Your heart & mind.
& it's okay to cry.
He's just emptying you out inside.
So He can fill you
With His Holy Spirit
& then you'll really thrive.

...[T]he Sovereign LORD says: My people, I am going to open your graves and bring you up from them; I will bring you back to the land of Israel. Then you, my people, will know that I am the LORD, when I open your graves and bring you up from them. I will put my Spirit in you and you will live, and I will settle you in your own land. Then you will know that I the LORD have spoken, and I have done it, declares the LORD.'"

-Ezekiel 37:12-14

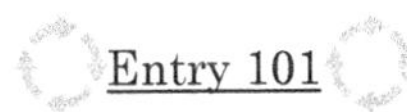

Entry 101

God I thank You for my cousin Twon
& I thank You for my dawg Key.
I pray that You show me what to do
In my community
So we don't have a repeat.
He replied
It starts with me.
Can't pour into nobody else
Until I'm free.

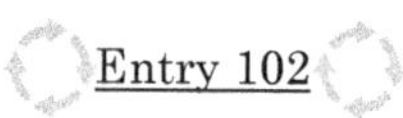

Entry 102

Thank You God
For protecting me
From what I couldn't see.
For helping me see
What I can be.
Thank You for seeing me
& never giving up on me
When everything was so heavy.

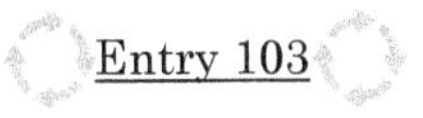

Entry 103

The depth to me
Is the depth in You.
My root is the color
Of blue.
For the first time
In forever
I have truly bloomed.
Understanding what it means
To be dedicated to You.
Just eight months ago
I felt so doomed.
& it showed
In my words & my moves.
I never felt stable
Or truly secure in my life.
Until now.
Always looking over my shoulder.
Anticipating others thinking
& living the way I did mentally.
In strife.
The world around me
Constantly caved in
Because of my world internally.
& waves of darkness
Consumed me
More than frequently.

But You
My God
Have opened me up.
Stuck by my side.
Held my hand
As You took me through
The excruciating process
Of emptying me.
You gave me the strength
To withstand the process
& not leave.
You lit my path
As I went inward
To search & clean.
My root is blue
Because of the depth of You.
Now I am floating
In this pool.
Peacefully.
Trusting You.
Totally.
You my God
Are my only hope.
My salvation.
My security.
My stability.
You have caused me to blossom.
Thank you♥

Blue signifies serenity, depth, wisdom & introspection.

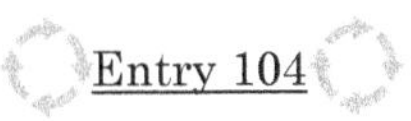

Entry 104

I watch you lay there
body bare
as you just stare
into your phone.
You've become more unaware
of your life's purpose.
Your impact.
Your emotions.
Your kids that are in
the next room
hoping
to get a piece of your love.
My eyes swell with tears
because this is one of
my greatest fears.
To lose you.
I have spent 22 years
living in you
& for you
so I think to myself
who would I be without you?
& prayed
I wouldn't have to find out.
But the truth is
I am dying
trying to sustain you.
Yet nothing I do
will ever be enough
to fill you up.

Because there are cracks
within you
that cause my love
to seep through
& the only one
who can fix that
is you.
So I must go on
begin living for me now...
I'm so terrified
that I won't survive
without the pieces
of your love.
Your touch...
but God told me that
He is enough.
I must release you now.
Take hold of Him.
& really allow my life
to begin again.
No longer can I use you
for identity.
I must find it in Him alone.
You put everything you have
into us.
My first real friend.
You protected us
& loved us
the best you could.
Did everything for us
you thought you should.

So I thank you
for the training
& the wisdom.
From these
I will never depart.
& as I learn to love
me for me
I pray my journey sparks
something similar within yourself
& in due time
we can again exchange hearts.
The right way.
With an abundance
of Love & light.
Doing what *God* calls right.
We will overcome this battle
of depression & trauma.
I promise mama.
I love you to life.
It's time for me to save me
so you can get right.

Entry 105

Why is it that
Every time we think
We've released something
A few months down the line
Of us releasing
It still has a finger
Latched onto us?
Or do I still have my grip
On it?
Him?
The downfall
& the brokenness
Of it all.
The pain
Of what I felt
The day I lost you.
& how I constantly lose you
Over & over again.
When a friend brings up your name.
Or when I see your picture
In a frame.
I promise you
I lose it all over again.
Why does this feel
Like a never-ending process
Of no progress?

Because as soon as
I take 5 steps into freedom
I'm pushed back
10 feet into the grave
Of bondage.
What am *I* doing wrong?
Why do these feelings arise?

I just saw you
With the guys
& then you were
With your girl.
Oops.
I mean your ex.
& I don't know why
But I'm really a mess.
Because even though
We're through.
Within a small place
In my heart
There's still room
For you.
For us.
Hoping it can be
What it was.
But better this time around.
Because we're both trying to build
With Christ as our ground.

But the truth is
I know that
I don't really want you
For you.
I'm sickly in love with the idea
Of you obsessing over me.
& what will I be
When that's no longer our story?
How can I let you go
When I've always had you?
What will I do
When it's no longer *me*
For you?
When there's absolutely
No more possibility
Of us two?
What do I do
When everything I thought to be true
Is shattered?
& I have to build again
From the bottom up
While emotionally battered.
Really from myself.
My own ways of thinking
& my life of sin
Before coming to the King.

I'm trying to get away
From that life of sin
& telling you
That we can no longer
Hang out as friends
Is the beginning
To the newness
For which I seek.
So I ask *myself*
For forgiveness
For being sad
For doing what's best
For me.
For us.
For the kingdom & community.
I have to release
My old way of thinking
& take full responsibility
For my life
& the direction
It takes.

Realizing that no one belongs
to you...

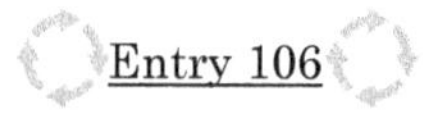

Entry 106

It's scary sometimes
When you look in the mirror.
Got me speechless
To be honest.
I don't want nobody
To see my face.
I'm messed up.
Wounded.
Selfish.
Judgmental.
As the Scripture goes
Apart from God
I have no good thing.
(Psalm 16:2)
I'm really feeling that
"I have no good thing"
Part quite intensely right now.
I guess it's to keep me humble.
But at times it makes me
Wanna quit.
I can't even stand to see
My own face
Sometimes...

But the fact that Jesus died for me
Knowing exactly who I would be.
Aware of every mistake I would make.
Every bit of self-doubt I would have.
Every person I would hurt.
He died for me.
So that I would have the chance to
Make my wrongs right.
It hurts to see the wrong decisions I've made.
But it makes my *whole* life
To see all the right decisions I can now make.
Thanks to Jesus.
His sacrifice that allotted reconciliation
To Love.
The fact that I'm no good.
But He's *SO* good.
I thank You Jesus
For keeping me around
Until I can get it right.
So that with You
I can spend my afterlife...♡

#LoverOfMySoul

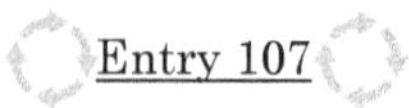

Entry 107

For so long
I misinterpreted Love.
I thought Love's nickname
was Happy.
I thought that with Love
Sadness could never
catch me.
& if I was Sad
I believed my Christian walk
reflected that I was cappin'.
There was no way
that I could be free
& experience Sadness.
Sadness to me
meant broken
& unusable.
Which coincides with worthlessness.
So clearly not beautiful.

Oh how I misinterpreted Love.
thinking that with Love
I should never be Sad.
According to my Dad
Sadness is supposed to
bring us closer.
Deeper in Love.
Sorrow should bring one
to "sorry."

Regret propelling her
to repent.
2 Corinthians 7:10
shows that in Love
I do have a friend.
One who saves me
in Sadness
again & again.
But if there was
no Sadness
Love could never be
my Savior...

Entry 108

God thank You
For where You have me today.
I experience the splendor.
Joy & peace.
Truly
I've never been so
At ease.
Most of my life
There was a spiritual drought.
Even though I followed You
I battled with so much doubt.
I doubted my abilities.
Your limitlessness.
Became hopeless
When talking about real Love
& what I once identified as
This "healing mess."
The world around me
Full of people lying.
Friends dying.
Uncontrollable crying.
I was ready to be done trying.
But then You put me in a place
Where I had no choice
But to pursue You.
Not only that.
You gave me people who were solid in You.
& then things really began to move.
My perspective of Love shifted.

Hope in my heart grew.
Because I truly began to see
Your Word & Spirit is all I need.
So I thank You God
For sustaining me.
Until Your blessings were plain to see.
Thank You for keeping me
When life told me certain situations
Would be the end of me.
Thank You for loving me
Past what everybody in the world
Could see.
The dirty me.
The confused me.
The selfish "B".
Ezekiel 16:14 says
It is because of You
That I have beauty.
& the final thanks
Will be for my testimony.
Thanks to You
I wish satan would test-Imani! :)

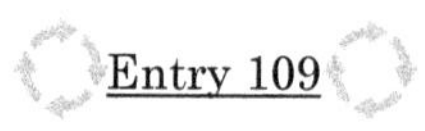

Entry 109

I'm looking for change
& I ain't talking 'bout a dime

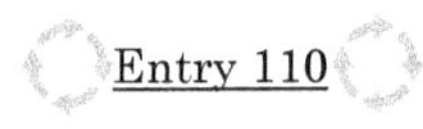

Entry 110

I told God
I'm ready to produce.

He replied,
"Okay.
But are you ready to purge?"

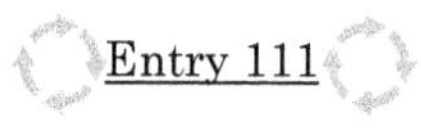

<u>Entry 111</u>

Sometimes you just gotta go in
with what you know
& allow yourself to grow
as you go

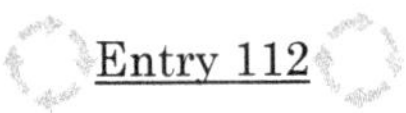

Entry 112

Reframe the pain
So that you don't
Go insane.
& understand
It was all for a
Spiritual gain.

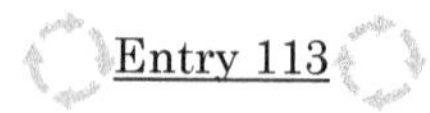

Entry 113

God You are the One.
Only You make me
dwell in safety.
God You are the One.
Yes You're the One
who made me.
True identity
You gave me.
No, no them people
can't save me.

You're the only One
I ever needed.
When I speak Your name
demons are defeated.
I'm no longer living life
with my energy depleted.
When people step to me
they gotta pay a fee, yeah.
They don't get the same access
since You delivered me
& I've been set free.
Only surround myself with people
who understand their divinity.
We walking in it.
Yeah it's in me.
This is the only way
we defeat the enemy.

If you rockin' with hate
you ain't no friend of me.
Yeah God got my back.
He's my covering.
He already told me
when He's watching over me
ain't no slumbering.
If you really woke
like my Father.
I said if you really woke
let me hear you holla, "Abba!"
We sacrificing daily.
It's a job, yeah.
Tryna clean up my sins
so I can make it
back to heaven again.
Got my hand to the plow
& I'm tryna keep my eyes focused.
Long as I keep my head in this Word
its power is potent!
I don't got time
to be moving slow &
I answer His call
because of my Bro, man–
His only Begotten.
Honoring the covenant.
Reconciliation with Love &
healing the wounds
below the surface.
I promise you man
this life is worth it.

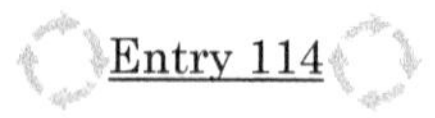

Entry 114

What you did was wrong.
You will get
your consequences.
God will dish them
out to you.
I must release you.
This weight of emotions–
Unforgiveness, anger, hurt.
It's all too heavy.
I cannot carry it
into my journey
to the Light.
Forgive me
for holding you hostage
& hindering the opportunity
for Love to abound
between us.
Forgive me
for not allowing you
to make mistakes
without judgment.
& forgive me
for withholding God's Love.
I, too, am sorry
for the sorrow
I caused you
while I was hurting, too.

Please
forgive me.

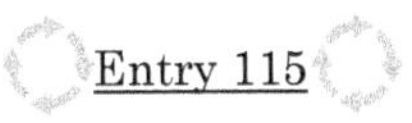

Entry 115

What happened happened
You control your reaction

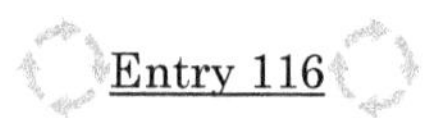

Entry 116

I could spend forever
With you.

But you were
Never mine to keep.

Whoever trusts in his own mind is a fool,
but he who walks in wisdom will be delivered.
-Proverbs 28:26 ESV

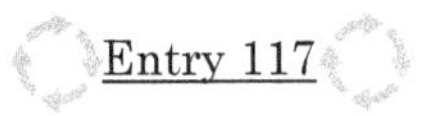

Entry 117

Thank You God
for showing me what to do.
Thank You that Your Love
sees me through
every waking issue.
Your Light informatively shines
on every misplaced pursuit.
You brighten the path of Life
& still
You allow *me* to choose.
The truth is
without You I am no good.
I'm irrationally emotional.
Highly fearful.
& I'm always in a mood.
Without You
I have no peace.

But with You
You are teaching me
I am everything
I need.
& I don't have to seek
externally.
Kanye said it best
we have everything we need.
You have me.
& I for you.
The perfect duo.

Thank You so much.
I Love You.

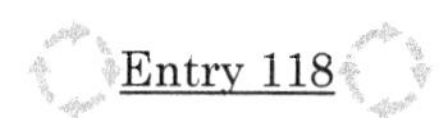

Entry 118

Thank You God
For always providing
A way.
A place.
A plate.
An escape.
Grace.
Mercy.
Thank You for providing
Funds & fun.

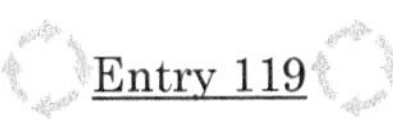

Entry 119

Thank you Jesus
for living in me
that I may be set free
from everything
that tries to consume
& overtake me

It is for freedom that Christ has set us free.
Stand firm, then, and do not let yourselves
be burdened again by a yoke of slavery.
-Galatians 5:1

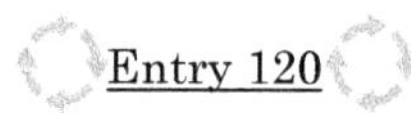

Entry 120

Good intentions
save nobody
without
Godly guidance

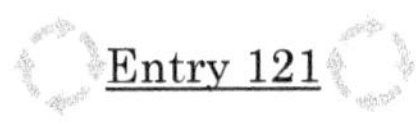

Entry 121

Fill me up God.
Without You
there is no me.
Without You
I don't have peace
or sanity.

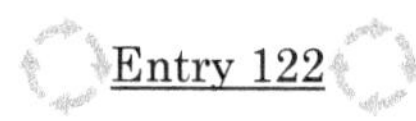

Entry 122

God's Kingdom is
The place to be.
Heaven sent.
No more
Jews & Gents.
With the Father.
Yeah He's so Divine.
Got my sister here
& my brother with me.
Growing spiritually.
We building something powerful.
For our children's children.
Breaking free
From satan's dimension.
Boutta have all of these demons
Under our dominion.

Entry 123

Holy Spirit
I am healed.
God
What You've given me
Is real.
I read Your Word
& I am filled.
You've surrounded me
With other humans
Who
Through Your Spirit
Have made me whole.
You continuously do
The impossible.
Led me to forgive
Years-old offenses
This year.
Surrounded me with
People I can trust
With my heart & Spirit.
I never thought
That day would come.
One held my hand
& with my other hand
I grabbed another one.
Last year
I suffered anguish
Alone.

This year
I gripped the hands
Of my truest loved ones
& we went to the Throne.
Thanks to this night
We've developed a bond
Rooted
Grounded
& deepened
In God.

They admit
They see me crack jokes.
Laugh & submit
To whatever the cause
Is at hand.
Yet they know I end the night
Alone.
Maybe even struggling
With hope.
They deem me
Strong.
Resilient.
Wise.
Admirable.
Authoritative.
Yet peaceful.
They have showed me
That no matter my past
God still loves me equal.
They say they love me.

They're grateful.
That if the bible study
They started
Was just for saving me
& helping me find the King
It was all worth it.
They say I've helped them
Persevere
& find hope.
My wise counsel helps them
To cope.
Experiencing everyone
With their passions & gifts
Come together & give
My Spirit a kiss.
Tiff playing the guitar.
Arroze performing the poem.
Jace straight affirming me.
& Johnny praying with passion.
So loudly.
Cain is intentional & gentle
In his expressions of love
For me.
Helping me to see
That my life has impacted
His family totally.

Leah broke me.
I really felt her love
Covering me.

She said how much
I've made her
A better woman.
Friend & disciple.
When people talk about
Christ 2020
That I am the example.
She says I've poured
So much into this
Church & body.
I am truly a vital piece
Of the puzzle.
She will pray for me.
Pray with me.
Be there whenever.

It took me back to
Our first solo hang out
Together.
We'd just lost
Loved ones
To gun violence.
Ugh.
The pressure.
& more than talking
We sat in the car
& just cried together.
Understanding
Each other's pain.

& silently acknowledging
The fact that neither of us
Had the right answers
To sort through it all.
But at least we had
The comfort of each other.

She has a way
With words
That truly consumes
The heart.
I never felt so loved.
God was speaking
To me via everybody.
That was Him.
Just in their bodies.
God embraced me tonight.
& this moment
I will never forget.

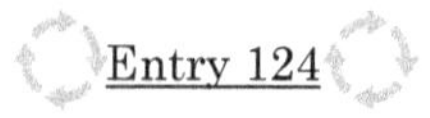

Entry 124

I am afraid
that I won't have people
alongside me to help me
bear the burdens
of life anymore.
I just came out of
one of the most trying years
of my life.
I didn't wanna live anymore.
& God sent them.
He spoke through them.
Loved through them.
Taught through them.
Healed through them.
& I opened my heart up to them.
& now things are changing.
Now things *have* to change.

& it hurts.
It scares me so much.

What happens next?
Do I end up alone again?
I know God is here.
But I mean alone
in the earth.
Like before.

I told myself
I wouldn't open
my heart up again
knowing that
everybody leaves.
Things change.
People die.
But I did it anyway.
Now I'm hurting.
Now I must mourn
yet another loss.

I felt like this would be forever.
I felt so secure
a few weeks ago.
Now my ground is shaking
& I just wanna stand still.
I'm not paralyzed
because I know God's Word.
But I wanna be paralyzed
to feel what I feel fully.
To be sad a little longer.
To elongate the shift.
It's been such a good time.
I don't want it to end.
I know I won't end up back
in nothingness because I've changed.
But the idea still comes & lingers
alongside fear.
Will everything that I've built internally
dissipate?
Will my identity in Christ
stand the test of time?
Will I be able to *truly*
weather this storm?

The last season of my life
I too was scared of the shift.
Who would I be
if Keykey died?

I thought
after Alexis called me at 5am
telling me he was in the hospital
having just been shot.
Who would I be
if I miss out on Shane again?
Who would I be
if I let him go again this time?
Will I be able to handle this
if I can't drink anymore?
Probably not.
Who am I now
that Twonnie is dead?
Who am I now
that I can no longer use
my mom for identity?

When I lost you
I felt like I lost everything.
My world was so shaken up.
I never wanna experience
a world-quake like that again.
I will close myself off
to getting attached
to anybody again
so I don't experience this
type of soul-crushing
mind-boggling feeling
again.

Always thinking,
"What could I have done
differently so that
this didn't have to happen to me?
Should I have stayed in the house
that night instead of longboarding?
Should I have stayed home
& not gone away to college?
Should I have given him
all of me the first time around
so that we
wouldn't be here now?
Struggling with trust issues
that eventually led to
the end of us?
Should I have just stayed
in the room more
& connected less?
So that I could still be living
with people who understand me?
Did I bring this shift
to my life?
Could I have stopped it
from coming?
Can I bear the pain
that comes with it?"
It's like the concept of thinking,
"I should have asked
for something cheaper
at Christmas
because now it's April
& we don't have any food
in the fridge."

In my heart I know
that one doesn't directly affect
the other.
But maybe it does.
My brain wants to find
any logical correlation
to fill in the grey areas.
& make it make sense...

#SOSI'mSlippingAgain

Entry 125

I know why the gear shifter
In my car broke.
I knew it the day it happened.
I didn't wanna acknowledge it
To my friends.
I was too ashamed.
Praising God faithfully.
Yet not wanting to move
When He says move.
Even now
Still struggling
With my feelings
On this matter.
Why can't I just
Lock them away
In a box
So I can obey
God's instruction
With no interruption?
I don't wanna second guess.
I don't wanna reconsider.
I just wanna move when
He tells me
& not feel a strain
Of disconnect
Because I've tied my soul
To people here on earth!

Sometimes I wish
I could live
Emotionless.
These emotions–
They're too intrusive.
I guess I got a choice
To make regardless.
It's time to put on
My work hat:
Disciple.
My life is not my own.

Every shift has brought better.
Brought me higher.
I just gotta get through the feels
to get there...

"The choice is yours." - GOD.

#MyChoiceIsMyPower

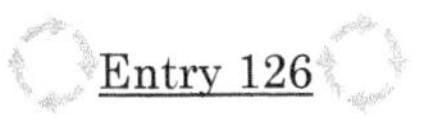

Entry 126

Sometimes I'm so careless.
Sometimes I'm so reckless.
So emotional & emotion-led.
& I lose myself.
Sometimes I lose myself
Intentionally.
Weighing the cost of
This level of gratification
Compared to my known
& established identity.
(Now I understand Esau)
Without You
I'm crazy enough
To think that feeling good
Is better than conforming
To the likeness of Christ.
Walking in the guaranteed peace
That You award me.
& after I lose me
You come & find me
& show me where I've lost me.
& You allow me to begin again.

Thanks Friend.

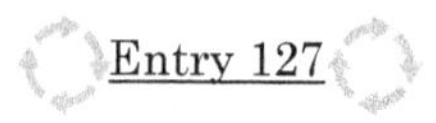

Entry 127

Jesus asked,
"Why are you afraid?
Do you still have no faith?"
(Mark 4:40)

I'm afraid because everything
Around me is changing
Constantly.
Persistently altering.
Right now
These emotions
Are faltering.
& yes at times
I feel as though
I'm losing my identity.
Imani without faith.
That's a non-existent entity.
Because you can't get one
Without the other.
So when I'm losing my faith
I'm losing myself.

I'm afraid because I must
Mourn another loss.
Last time I was here
I lost myself.

& the worst part
Of this ask of You Lord
Is they're not dead
This time.
So my faithlessness
Has led me to anticipate
Losing them again & again.
Every day I see them
& I can no longer hang.
No longer can I engage
Because what has become
Of our relationship
Has come close
To putting a hedge
Between us.
You & I.
Knowing this
Why does this heart
& these eyes
Continue to cry?

I'm afraid
Because everything changes
Except You.
& every time I approach You
I forget to properly distinguish
The two.
Everything vs. You.
Because You are everything.
To be true.

I'm faithless
At times
Because my flesh questions,
"What makes *You*
So different?
This changes into *that*
& *that* changes into *this*
& as soon as I think
I've gotten these
Changes & patterns
Down pat
It switches up again.
Just like that.
& here You are
Saying You are exempt
From that law."

But the truth is
I know deep down
Every time this shift has come
I've had to walk
By faith.
Not by what I saw.
I must keep my eyes
On You
To weather this storm.
You are my only
Sure security.
Unchanging God.
Everlasting Love.
Unfailing Kindness.

& I can't continue to
Run & hide
From You.
Even when my flesh
Questions the validity
Of You...

After he has suffered,
he will see the light of life and be satisfied;
by his knowledge my righteous servant will justify many,
and he will bear their iniquities.
-Isaiah 53:11

#impatientlywaiting...

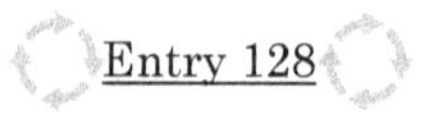

Entry 128

God Your Word
Is the only thing
That sustains me.
It's so easy
To become
A slave
To my selfish desires
& the luxuries in life
That keep me complacent.
But I wasn't placed here
For comfort.
No
Wrong "C".
I was placed here
For Christ
& that He may
Be seen in me.
So if that means
Giving it all up
So that You will be
Lifted on high
I'll do it again & again.
Your Word
Is my instruction.

My guidance.
My clarity.
If I didn't have it
I'd be in bondage.
Day in & day out
For eternity.
There'd be no such thing
As peace.
No clean, crisp air
To breathe.
I'd suffocate myself
In pursuit of
My selfish desires
& not You.
Your Word reminds me
Of Your faithfulness
& Your perfection.
You didn't give up on Peter
After he denied
The Holy One.
Not even after
The 3rd time.
You prepared him
By telling him
He would fall.

& You allowed
The Holy Spirit
To descend on him
In further chapters.
Flaws & all.
Alpha & Omega.

The beginning
& the end.
My instructor.
My truest friend.

With You
There is a guaranteed greatness.
No matter how it may
Sometimes feel.
In Acts 4
Peter & John were jailed
For teaching & healing.
In the name of Jesus...
By *Your* instruction.
If it was me
That may have been
End of discussion.
But a couple lines later
I learned that
Because of their faithfulness
The number of disciples grew
To about 5,000.

5,000 souls
Finding a Light
In the midst of their darkness.
5,000 souls
Finding a resolve
To every unanswered question
They've been imprisoned by.
5,000 souls
Finding a home.
5,000 souls reaching bliss
Inside their own dome.

Bc of *Your* instruction.

Your perfection.
Their obedience.

God
Your Word
Preserves my life.
Without it
Like Nicki Minaj
I'm not living right
Cause You're not
By my side.
Your Word teaches me
How to live in obedience
& how to move selflessly.
Even if it hurts.

As I pursue righteousness
I will be filled.
You are truly
The best thing
That's ever happened
To me.
Without You
I have no good thing.
& with You by my side
I am everything.
Forever prospering.
In my emotions.
In my decisions.
You are the Great
I Am.

Thank You for rebirthing me♡

Turn my heart toward your statutes
and not toward selfish gain.
Turn my eyes away from worthless things;
preserve my life according to your word.
-Psalm 119:36-37

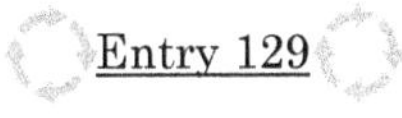

Entry 129

In order to build
what God has for you
you have to
have the strength
to stand apart

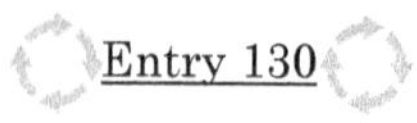

Entry 130

My whole being aches.
From my body.
To my soul.
& mind.
This is what
God was standing
In front of
For me.
& I still just had to
Go & see.
Silly me.
I pray I never
Get caught in this
Same trap again.
I'm so tired of it.
& this.
I feel 15 all over again.
18.
20.
Now I'm 23
In the same hot seat.
Damn man
I just wanna leave!

I just gotta do better.
Trust myself
& the King...

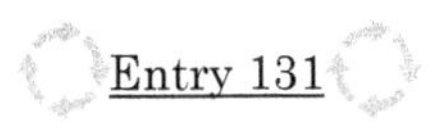

Entry 131

Just because you do something wrong
Doesn't mean you're not living right

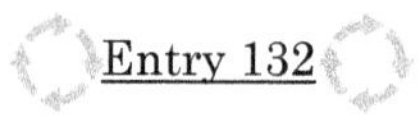

Entry 132

The rain hurts.
But it purifies.

It's inconvenient.
But it purifies.

If you let it.

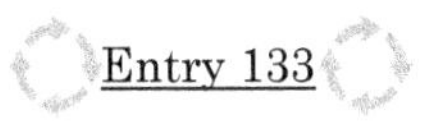

Entry 133

Forced to normalize something
That was not normal.
Thoughts.
Behaviors.
Energies.

Forced to enter & accept
Environmental changes.
Some without notice
Or discussion.

Forced to focus on something
I did not agree to.

I don't know what's happening
But I know something is happening.

I am not oblivious.
I am not crazy.

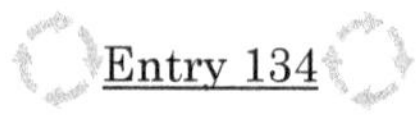

Entry 134

What did you really want from me?
You clouded my judgment
& you confused me!
It was only clear to see
Once I left your vicinity.
I would've never did you
How you did me.
It hurts because I really tried
This time to choose
Intentionally.
Give my God-given best
To those surrounding me.
I did so much right.
Yet I still did some things wrong.
I should've left the first time
God told me.

"But your eyes and your heart
Are intent only upon your own dishonest gain,
And on shedding innocent blood,
And on practicing oppression and extortion."
-Jeremiah 22:17 NASB

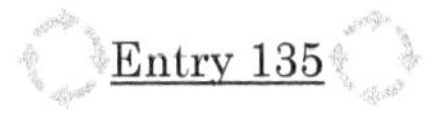

Entry 135

It's lonely
When you got standards.
You see everybody out there
Entertained.
Engaged.
& "happy".
But what you can't see physically
Is their inauthenticity.
Their compromise of self
& identity.
For friends & romantic partners
& things that aren't really
Meant to be...

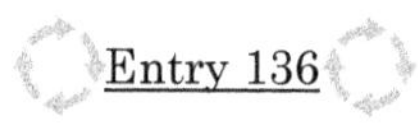

Entry 136

Life without God...
A whole headache
& a lifetime of
Heartbreak

Entry 137

It's sad to see
How you run
From the Light
Of liberation.
Shacking up in the shadows
Of death.
It's sad to watch you
Settle for less than
God's best
For you.
That which you're entitled to.
Satan has slipped his way
Into your psyche
& coerced you to compromise
Your true self
In exchange for all else.
It was never worth it
& it will never be.

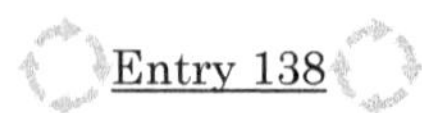

Entry 138

You will be hated by everyone because of me,
but the one who stands firm to the end will be saved.
-Matthew 10:22

They hate me
Because
They hate themselves
& how much my courage
Sheds light on
Their cowardness.
They hate me
Because
They hate the fact
That they can't get a grip
On their flesh
For long enough
To be consistently
Led & fed
By Holy Spirit.
They think I have
Some sort of
Magical power
Or personal
Divine impartation
From the Holy One.

The thing is
I do.
But the magic is
They do too.

See I'm just a man.
Like you.
But I've sacrificed myself
In order for God to lead
My every move.
Light cannot dwell
Where darkness is.
So once God came into me
See I had to let go
Of some things.
He's just waiting on you
To let go too.
So He can bestow
Glory on you.
& reveal
What He *really* created
You to do.
Until then
You will wreck every life
You come in contact with.
Including your own.
Because you're not able
To move from a genuine place
Of sincere Love.
Authenticity.
& real resolve.
Unstable in all that you do.
At this point
I have compassion on you.
& now I understand
Why Jesus said
To pray for those
Who persecute.

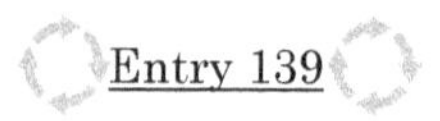

Entry 139

See
God can't bless
Who you pretend to be.
& Ima be me
Even if it gets me hated.
Even if it gets me killed
Out in these streets.
Cause I'd rather be
At odds with you
Than myself & the Spirit.
Sick of being frustrated.
Tired of giving myself to people
Who simply take advantage.

I gotta keep reminding myself
That I've been consecrated
Before, during, & after
This experience.
Christ is still here.
He's still with me.

"If only my anguish could be weighed
and all my misery be placed on the scales!
It would surely outweigh the sand of the seas—
no wonder my words have been impetuous.["]
-Job 6:2-3

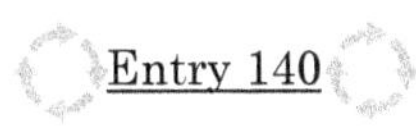

Entry 140

Disobedience breeds destruction
Deception breeds death

#trapped

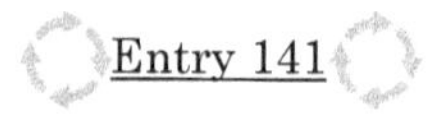

Entry 141

I just wanna be alone.
Yet not lonely.

I've lost me again.

Will I ever shake this loneliness?
Will I always desire to be
In a man's arms when I feel it?
Will I ever be genuinely happy?
Will it ever last?

I'm tired.
Of me.
These desires.
This brokenness.
My messiness.

I am so tired.

Hear my voice when I call, LORD;
be merciful to me and answer me.
-Psalm 27:7

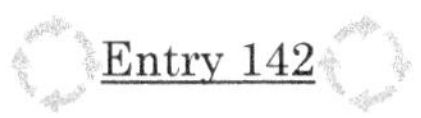

Entry 142

I'll always love you.

But you won't always
Own a piece of my soul.

Another one
Bites the dust.
Yeah it sucked
Because I ran amok
Without my number One
Guider & Friend.
Father & Man.
No one to really blame
But me.
My filthy rags of righteousness.
Thankfully
God lets me
Begin again.
With wisdom & ease.
I'll get it right one day.
& when I do

you'll no longer own
a piece of my soul.

All of us have become like one who is unclean,
and all our righteous acts are like filthy rags;
we all shrivel up like a leaf,
and like the wind our sins sweep us away.
-Isaiah 64:6

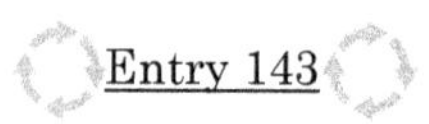

Entry 143

Some days
I'm so afraid to
Face the day...

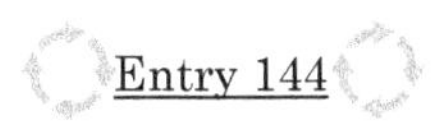

Entry 144

I ache for the older version
Of myself.
Who I was
Before you broke me.
& I can't seem to release
That pain
Because what comes next
Is uncertain.

#afraid

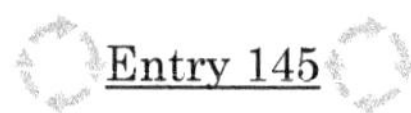

Entry 145

It's time
To crawl out
Of this dark
Cozy hole
Of suffering...

I think I can.
I think I can.

Entry 146

As I breathe in
The air
I can feel You here.
I close my eyes
& I can be anywhere.
My imagination
Gives me limitlessness.
No matter where I'm at
I am right there
With You.
Just one prayer away.
One thought geared
Toward You.
It brings teardrops to my face
To understand
I'm fully known & Loved
By You.
& to know
That I can access You
No matter what I've done
Or been through.

Thank You for
Choosing to be anywhere
In the world with me.♡

Entry 147

They hate to see you
With the ball
They dropped

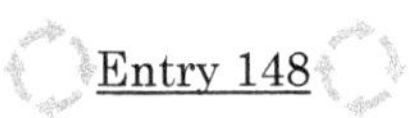

Entry 148

I wanna run again.
Things are seemingly
Closing in on me.
I don't feel secure enough.
Strong within myself.
& I wanna run again.

& then authority sets in.
Showing me that
I don't have to run again
Because Jesus is my friend.
He'll hold me tight.
Make sure everything
Works out just right.

I wanna run.
But I don't have to
This time.

Entry 149

Aunts, uncles, cousins.
Grandmas & a great grandma.
Barely any men in the picture.
I wonder where I come from.
Beyond those who are still here.
Those who have transfigured.
Transcended.
& are now elsewhere.
I feel like the black sheep.
But I know somewhere down deep
They're here.
In me.
The painters.
The poets.
Those who are so introspective
It hurts.
I know there are more like me.
There just had to be!
Because I didn't come out of thin air
With these talents & gifts.
Many of which
I would've never even picked.
There's a heaviness that comes
Tied to every writer & poet.
A loneliness that only God
Truly understands.
But it births a burst
Of hope & unity.
To know that we humans
Do not suffer alone.

Sometimes I wonder
Where did I come from?
Where was my praying grandma?
The one who gathered all the family
In strength?
Or my great aunts & uncles?
Who should have taught me
About the salvation
& righteousness of the Lord?
Those who shared their scars
So I wouldn't have to endure.
I wonder who in my lineage
Was a painter.
Was she beautiful?
Was he heartfelt?
Could you sense the pain
& emotion in their eyes?
Was painting their saving grace
In this rugged race?
Did they ever dream of running away?
Becoming a full-time painter
As their escape?
Was there anyone in my lineage
Who didn't escape with drugs?
I been tryna do it differently
But I can't see another way.
I wonder if there was ever
Anyone like me in my lineage
& if so
I wish I could ask them for
Advice & encouragement
On my journey of becoming...

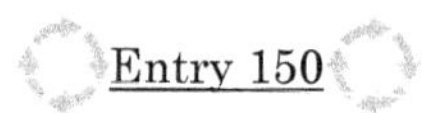

Entry 150

I'm not even looking at the sky.
I'm somewhere else
In my mind...
If something crashed into me
Right now
I don't think I'd feel a thing...

#numb

Entry 151

I knew
Pain could hurt.
But I've never admitted
To myself
How good it could feel.
As I ache
I can seemingly go away.
Vanish into the abyss.
Hidden from all responsibilities
As depression takes precedence.
Falling back into the familiarity of it.
No longer having to fight for freedom
Day in & day out.
I now have a reason to tap out.

#seeminglyjustified

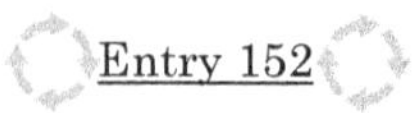

Entry 152

Life doesn't stop
For anybody.
Yet I stand still.
No movement.
Not even this heart of mine
It seems.
In hopes that
Everything within
Will come to a halt.
No matter how many times
My heart
Has been broken
Every time feels
Like the first.
Like I didn't remember
Pain this deep
Existed.
The way
My body aches.
The way
My stomach turns.
The way my eyes cry
Effortlessly.
Not only is my soul weak.
This body
That hosts it
Quivers.
Nothing can be
Held fast here.

All wants to come
Bursting from the seams.
With every bite of food
I feel nauseous.
Every place I drive pass
That we've shared
A piece of me
Internally chips away.
& with every thought
Of you...
What was.
What became of us.
& what broke us.
I wish I could shut off
Every organ in me
& just turn the lights out...

Answer me quickly, O LORD!
My spirit fails!
Hide not your face from me,
lest I be like those who go down to the pit.
-Psalm 143:7 ESV

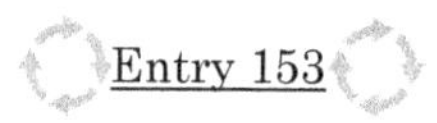

Entry 153

The little girl in me
She's looking for redemption...
Subconsciously it's happening
Holy Spirit is revealing & dismantling

Maybe if the Love was restored in you
It would pour into me
Maybe if I pour here
I'll receive some sort of reciprocity...

What is Love really supposed to look like?
What is Love really supposed to be?
Getting it wrong likely.
But what's new?
That's just like me...

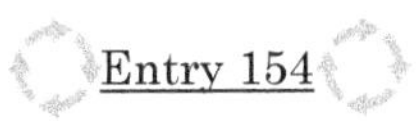

Entry 154

You *had* cancer.
You *have* asthma.
& yet I watch you
Still
Take your daily
Smoke breaks...
Faithfully...
As quick as my flesh
Wants to judge you
I am no different
Than you.
I stay in unhealthy
Relationships
Past their ending
Being long overdue.
Slowly but surely
Taking the very breath
Out of my lungs.
Suffocating my Spirit.
Killing my soul.
We humans
Do very foolish things
In an attempt to escape
Life's pain.

While simultaneously
Bringing more pain into
Our being.

#SearchingForFreedomAgain

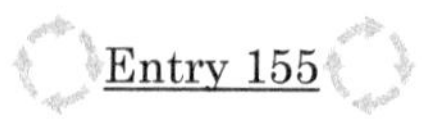

Entry 155

Jesus heals.
Without Jesus
My heart will remain
Broken.

We all Love
& lose.
Open up
& get bruised.
Not every time.
But it will always happen.
Somehow.
Through someone.
In this broken
Broken world.

& this is why
I have to connect
Daily
To Christ.

Because Jesus heals.
Without Jesus
My heart will remain
Broken.

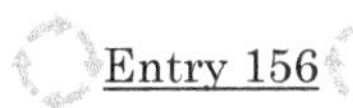

Entry 156

If an enemy were insulting me, I could endure it; if a foe were rising against me, I could hide. But it is you, a man like myself, my companion, my close friend, with whom I once enjoyed sweet fellowship at the house of God, as we walked about among the worshipers. My companion attacks his friends; he violates his covenant. His talk is smooth as butter, yet war is in his heart; his words are more soothing than oil, yet they are drawn swords.
-Psalm 55:12-14, 20-21

I'm struggling
to admit to Him
that I'm confused
on what to do.
How to handle
these emotions
& my view...
He was my friend.
I don't have a clue
how to accept
this new truth.

It's in the Scriptures
that He so graciously
allowed me
to find solace in knowing
my Spirit isn't blind.
I know what's going on
partially.

Just gotta get this mind
& these emotions
on the same wave.

This is what I need
His Spirit for.
It *is* conflicting.
Life *is* confusing.
People mislead.
People disappoint.
& I'm still left here
with these emotions
& strongholds
to sort.
He loves me.
He loves me not.
His lips say one thing
while his heart does not.
God is showing me
how easy it is
to be deceived.

It's not necessarily
solely a me thing.
It's an us-without-Him-thing.

Entry 157

They taught me everything
They could.
Gave me everything
That was good.
Like how to ride the waves
So I don't get overtaken.
I guess I just never
Expected them to become one...
Instead of being shocked
About it
I pray I learn to accept it.
The fact that I lost
Best friends again
Because God wasn't
In it.
Removed from their hearts.
Seemingly totally vanished.
It hurts.
But I don't have to
Close myself off
Because with God involved
My next *will be* much better
Than my last.

I must release you.
The pain you caused me.
Even some days
the good you brought me...

Because I know
Things'll never
Be that way again.
Things'll never
Be the same again.

It was fun while it lasted.
It was fun
Until it wasn't anymore.
I wish you God
& healing.
So you'll never hurt another
In this same way.

Please God
Let us be done with
Destroying others.

The Lord is close to the brokenhearted
and saves those who are crushed in spirit.
-Psalm 34:18

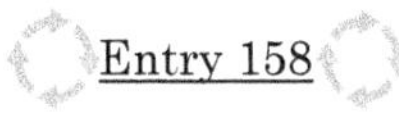

Entry 158

Hope deferred kills
The human soul.

Don't let your hope
Become deferred.

Hope deferred makes the heart sick,
but a longing fulfilled is a tree of life.
-Proverbs 13:12

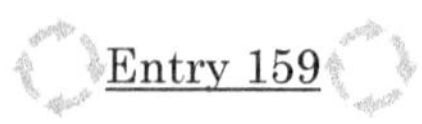

Entry 159

I thought I'd moved through
This grieving process.
Struggled through each stage.
Denial.
Anger.
Bargaining.
Depression.
Acceptance.

Yet here I am
At 10pm
Coming to grips with the fact
That I lost my best friend.
My favorite friend.
It hurts that it hurts.
& that hurt leaves me
Struggling to speak my truth.

I really lost my best friend...
Again...
The one I could
Confide in
About my issues.
The one I could cry on
& she'd thoughtfully go
& grab me tissues.

The one who'd massage
My back when I had cramps
& rub my skin
When I battled eczema flare-ups.
The one I could laugh with
Until we had tears
Streaming down our faces.
We woke up
& pursued the Lord together.
Fasted.
Painted.
Wrote poetry & shared it.
We teamed up.
Worked out
& wrestled our flesh.
She challenged me
When my thoughts were a mess.
She affirmed me
When insecurities grew in influence.
When I wanted to tear myself down
She'd build me up.
With the Word of the Lord.
I never had a friend like that before.

Whenever you saw me
You'd see her.
If she was somewhere else
I wasn't that far.

& if you questioned either of us
About the others' whereabouts
We were able to answer.
Without a doubt.
I felt confident because of that.
Confident that she had my back.
She was my best friend.
No one else's.
I cherished that.
I valued her
& exemplified that.
No question if I was willing
To bang out behind her.
I would go to war with whoever.
That was really my girl.
My sister.

In a world where
I've always felt misunderstood.
For the first time
In forever
I felt truly Loved.
By a woman.
By a sister.
With a childlike spirit.
Who also possessed wisdom.

How did we lose that?
Where did we misstep?

Is there any way
We could confront this
& go back?
Try again?
I've struggled to admit it.
But I miss my friend.
You made me feel so safe
At a point in time.
How could you break my heart?
I'm willing to forget it all & move on.
I need you by my side.
I want you there.

I'll never have the courage
To say that to your face.
My heart is afraid
Of letting you know
How much I love you.
How much I believe I need you.
Because you crossed the line.
How could you?
Selfishness forced me
To leave you.
You ensnared me
As if I was food.
To you, I was some sort of
Remedy for something
That should've been kept
In your bedroom.

Now we're through.

Everything is so confusing.
I don't know what to do.
How am I supposed to feel?
Which feelings are supposed to be here?
& which aren't?
If you can't be here
I just have to figure it out.
How to move on
Without you.
& verbalizing this agony.
This desire.
Does nothing for either of us two...

Lord please set this desire on fire.
I don't wanna see it.
I don't wanna hear about it.
I don't wanna face it any longer...

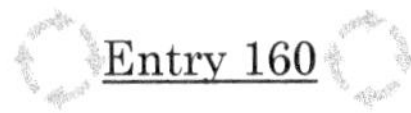

Entry 160

-What if I'm never enough for anyone to stay?

-Oh! But what about Jesus who stays?

-Why is it that sometimes that just doesn't feel like enough?

– internal conversations with myself

Entry 161

It's not until
the world goes dark
that I realize
how deeply
I'm hurting.
There are no lights on
around me.
Nobody to see my face
fully.
I can simply implode
in my bedroom
all alone.
Just God & I.
No eyes watching
to make sure
I have it all together.
That I'm playing my best cards
right.
No.
No one watching.
Critiquing & judging me.
Even as I judge myself
because their eyes will
eventually rest
on me & my results.

There's something so frightening
yet satisfying
about the dark.

I can be the ugly
broken me.
With no one else
to see.

But what if
they never see...the real me?
The broken me?
Then who will empathize with me?
Who will hear my cries
& come make sure I'm alright?

It's all so conflicting!
Sometimes I just need a break.
From this mind & this life.
Maybe because
I'm trying to figure it all out
before it even happens.
Thinking my way through it
instead of feeling my way through it.
Hoping my thinking
will allow it to be
less of a mess.

Because when you're so meticulous
& care about every little detail
who wants a dirty anything?
It's safer for everyone involved
if it's less of a mess.
When your mind works
in rules & regulations
shouldn't there be a precise formula
to achieving sanity & freedom?

#perfectionismiskillingme

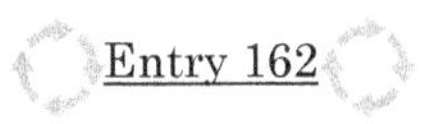

Entry 162

I am so desperate
to get through this part
of my life because
I am hurting
so badly.
Scared to be alone.
Yet the desire
to be my myself
is so dire.
To just break down & think.
Take my mind
to the better memories
of us.
Ruminate.
Figure out how this happened
& how I can get out of this.
It just doesn't make linear sense.
It's all so messy.
Yet I can't afford to leave it
for another to slip & fall in...

So I suck it up.
Turn the lights back on
& get back to work...

#healingme

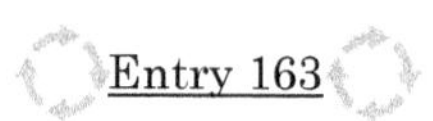

Entry 163

Every moment
Is supposed to be
Transformative.
Every moment
Is supposed to be
Divine.
Every moment
Is supposed to be
More than a moment.
Because You are
My King.

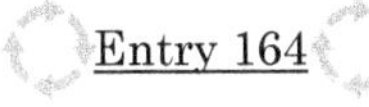

Entry 164

Freedom.
I hear it.

Freedom.
I feel it.

Freedom
To Love.
Freedom
To learn.

Freedom
To fall.
Freedom
To burn.

I wanna burn
Endlessly
For You Lord
& all that You
Stand for.

I wanna Love
& be Loved.

I wanna
Sow & reap
Righteously.
At the expense
Of me.

See because my flesh
Is weak
& it causes me
To seep
In waters
I'm not even supposed
To be.

I'm called
To walk on these
Waters.
Not sink.

Freedom is You.
I've gotten a taste!
& I pray that You're
Not through
Pouring into
Your willing vessel.

Those days are over.
Being sad & blue.
You've made me
A Mighty Warrior.
An overcomer.
A woman of power
& authority.

So when Sadness comes
I demand it not stay.

When Unforgiveness
Tries to come & play
Its foolish little games
I bind it up.

Like Jesus
In Matthew 22
I don't got time
To play!

Lives are at stake.
Lives are on the line.
First & foremost
Mine.
& I will not succumb
Any longer
To the enemy's
Wicked schemes
When I am a part of
The Divine.
The Most High.
My Truest King ♡

Entry 165

God is my first friend.
Anybody who helps
Walk me toward my purpose
Is my friend too.
The good & the bad.
Jesus called Judas friend
In Matthew 26:50
Right after He came out of Gethsemane.
Praying.
Begging the Lord, "Take this cup from Me!"
Job prayed for his friends
Who led him astray
During his darkest hour.
& was blessed with double of everything he lost
Moments after.
The good & the bad
I will thank.
Because they each walked me
Closer toward the cross
To fulfill my purpose
Of being a living sacrifice.
Those ignorant.
Those wise.
Those humble.
& those with pride.

When will we realize
God's standards of anything
Is not that of this world's?

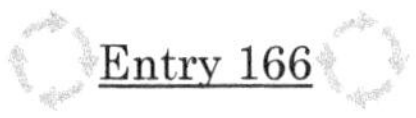

Entry 166

With each wave that comes
It pushes me back to the start.
The shore.
The shallows.
Where it's safe.
But in that place
It doesn't build faith.
& with every pushing wave
I have to make
The conscious effort
To stride again.
Stronger.
Releasing the fear & doubt
That I won't be able to win
Against the next
Incoming wave.
Each wave is consistent.
Persisting no matter
If I was able to overcome
The previous one or not.
They're just doing their job.
Being waves.
Flowing in & out.
Each ocean wave
Like a wave of emotion.
Trying to crash over me
& sweep me off my feet.
Leave me beat.
After I go under
I come up looking around.
Embarrassedly.
To see if anyone else
Saw me take this defeat.

But I can't look around
Or cry for too long.
Because the next wave's
On her way.
& again
She crashes over me.
Until I begin to piece
This pattern together
& see how this is gonna be.
Ride the waves.
Know when to jump with them.
& know which ones to go under.
There's a technique to it.
Don't *stay* emotional over what's happening.
Just learn the game.
The waves.
They come.
They go.
Some high.
Some low.
But nevertheless
They come.
& eventually
They go.
Don't run from them
Or you will be overtaken.
Learn how to ride the waves
So that you may enjoy your experience
In life's beach.

#RegainingMyStrength

Entry 167

For our struggle is not against flesh and blood, but against the rulers, against the authorities, against the powers of this dark world and against the spiritual forces of evil in the heavenly realms.
-Ephesians 6:12

I stand against the majority.
No wonder why
I feel lonely.
Rulers & authorities.
Those who govern
This community
& corrupt most
Into loonies.
I stand for freedom.
Personal expression
In Christ.
Individuality.
I don't ever wanna be bound
To another yoke of slavery.
The only chains I need
Are those that are gold
& those wrapped around my feet
Engraved with a "C".
Christ is King.
& I am His slave
Until the end.

So if that means
I must endure
Periods of loneliness
It's all worth it.
Father God said
He'd never leave
Nor forsake me.
So I'm never alone.
Even when I feel lonely.

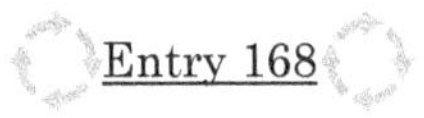

Entry 168

Lord
Help me
To move
When You say
Move.
To trust
That You
Have my best interest.
That You got me
Even if You're leading me
To Gethsemane...
To die to me.
Remind me
That it is to save
Many.

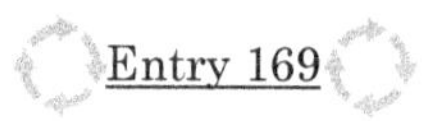

Entry 169

I was a lost little girl
Looking for God in him.
Desperately looking for
An anchor.
He did not anchor me
To life.
He anchored me
To death.
& when I sank
He walked away
& kept on living.

Some spiritual shepherd
You were...

"Anyone who withholds kindness from a friend
forsakes the fear of the Almighty.["]
-Job 6:14

Entry 170

Thank You that I didn't lose my laughter.
Thank You that I didn't lose my smile.
Thank You that I didn't lose my sense of humor.

Pain changes you.
But it doesn't have to be the end of you.
Just the end of one version of you.

Entry 171

The pain
Makes it most memorable.
Unforgettable.
The lessons of life.

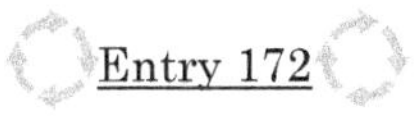

Entry 172

Thank You that You invite me
to redeem the pain.
Rename the pain.

I now pray
intently
before connecting with anyone.
No longer so innocently naive.
Wanting to cling
to every person who deems themself
as a part of Your being.
"Christian."
Comes in many forms.
Some authentic.
Many far from.
I pray that whomever
I come in contact with.
Whomever I decide to share space
& heart with.
That they are a true servant
& student of You.
I pray that we are able
to minister to each other.
I pray for the discernment
to see & know
who
in their heart
is just here for show.

I now know
what it means
to truly be one with You.
First & foremost.
No longer can I put
relationships & things
ahead of You
& be confused
about why trouble
is now causing me doom.
When I've taken You
out of Your proper place.
& I thank You that
I'm not able to rest in that.
Thank You for teaching me
how to read the signs
& recalibrate.

This walk called life
is about
You & I.
Her & You.
Him & You.
Nothing we do
will ever truly feel cool
if we aren't choosing to walk
in that truth.
Friends come.
Seasons shift.
Relationships & occupations
chip.

But what remains
is You.
& only You.
All things & people given
are simply gifts.
However long You decide
we get them
is up to You.
& I have to be in alignment
with that.
I need to be in agreement
with that.
No matter how much
I've come to love "it".
Because the Gift Giver
is whose Love
truly transforms me.
The Giver of the gifts
is who continually
vouches for me.
The God of gracious gifts
knows what I need
& what I can no longer handle.
He removes the gift
when I begin to allow it
to dismantle
who I am in Christ Jesus
& what I've been created for.

So no matter how much it hurts
Holy Spirit *please* close that door.
& remind me again
that my truest friend
will always be You.
Because after everything
has faded away
still You remain.
Thank you♡

I no longer call you servants, because a servant does not know his master's business. Instead, I have called you friends, for everything that I learned from my Father I have made known to you.
-John 15:15

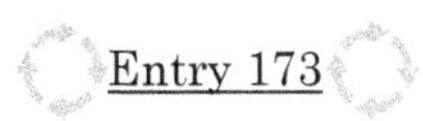

Entry 173

With God
There's a constant peak
As long as I seek.

#REALRelationshipGoals

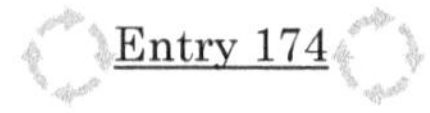

Entry 174

Wow.
Imagine losing that.
It's like losing
The very breath
In your lungs.
But God shows you
You can breathe
Without it.
Yet
In the same sense
God gives us this gift
Of intimacy...
The ability for someone else
To become a part of your soul.
That the moment you lose them
You've lost you, too.
The whole of you.
Even if just for a little while.
Until you're willing to hear
His calm voice remind you
"It's all one big gift...
On borrowed time."
Life is a very...
Intense
Contradictory...
Balance.
Life can only truly
Be experienced.
We don't understand it.

Understanding is a gracious gift
Of the Holy Spirit.
To be able to make sense
Of it all.
The coming together
& the falling apart.
The crops & cuts
& tears of the pictures.
The smiles & laughs
& innocent uncontrollable
Kiddy giggles.
Life's unforgettable moments.
The moments
You'll always laugh about.
The moments
You'll always cry about.
The way
That the human heart
Is perpetually penetrated.
Yet fiercely
Continues to beat.
What another gift
Of the Spirit–
Eternal life.
When I accepted Christ
As my Lord & Savior
I was made a promise–
That I would never
perish again.

I was gifted
Eternal life.
(John 3:16)
So although
There may be moments
I *feel* like I'm dying.
My Spirit's heart
Will never stop
Beating.
No matter what
I experience.
God *will* give me
Beauty for ashes.
I just gotta stick around
Long enough
To see the manifestation
Of it.

[A]nd provide for those who grieve in Zion—
to bestow on them a crown of beauty instead of ashes,
the oil of joy instead of mourning, and a garment of praise instead of a spirit of despair. They will be called oaks of righteousness, a planting of the Lord for the display of his splendor.
-Isaiah 61:3

Entry 175

I often feel like
I'm too much
For people.
Too much woman.
Too much emotion.
Too much depth.
Too much devotion...
But that's how God made me.
& that "too much"
Is the very passion
That saves me.
God gives us
Special individualized
Gifts.
But because they don't look like
A gift we would personally
Ask for
We don't recognize
The gift.
I'm beginning to recognize
My gift is my depth
& devotion.
Yes.
I feel deeply.
I feel everything.
Deeply.
& most times
It scares the heck out of me.

But God said
He'll never leave.
So with that
I believe I can
Take on anything.
No longer do I need
To numb myself
To bypass the pain.
Or shun myself
For wanting to share
A Love that has depth.
This is me
& only *I* can do the best
At being me.

Praise God.

#LearningToLoveTheRealMe

Entry 176

The very thing
That we try
To push off
& stuff away
Is the very thing
That You've
Blessed us uniquely with.
My sensitivity
Is my power.
My ability to feel
Deeply
& cry easily.
It's my power.
I've spent my whole life
Trying to turn it off
With alcohol.
Weed.
Superficial relations
With men & friends.
Being consumed
By anger.
Allowing my heart
To become cold & hard.
I tried so hard
& so long
To numb myself.
I was so afraid
To feel deeply
Because I thought
I'd actually die
If I did.
I didn't know how
To do it.

How to manage it.
How to just *be.*

Your Holy Spirit
Taught me.♥

Now
When I feel it coming
I just mentally prepare.
The internal dialogue–
"Alright everybody
Give room for the tears
& the feels.
Let them have their moment
Completely.
So they can come & go
Fully.
If not
They'll *make* a way
& probably at
The worst time possible."

I cry.
Outside.
In the car.
At events.
In church.
During conversations.
In therapy.
I cry.

I now give myself
Permission to be
Who God created me to be.

I am soft.
I am sensitive.
That's how God made me.
& I am grateful.
I feel so close to Him
When I cry.
I feel Him right there with me.
Comforting me.
Listening to me.
Fully attentive
To my heart's needs.
& once it's over
It's over.
No more lingering.
I'm not trying
To randomly suppress it
Throughout the day
With unhealthy distractions.

No more anxiety
When it randomly comes up
Anymore.
I am free.
Free to be me
Unapologetically.
I am free enough to cry.
No.
I am not weak.
No longer do I need
To hide
What resides
In this heart of mine.
She is sensitive
& she has needs.

She is so faithful
& strong.
A true warrior.
She deserves
To get her needs met.
She meets the needs
Of others effortlessly.
No question about
Meeting others' needs
Carries on for long.
So I vow
To make room
For her
To have her own throne.
To rest.
Cry out.
& reset.
Because this journey
Is hard & long.

But she's gonna make it.
That's how God ordained it.

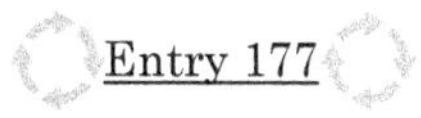

Entry 177

When I sit idly
These thoughts
Cloud me.
The memories
Taunt me.
Undoubtedly
They speak.
Months have passed
Yet the experiences remain
Clear as day.
The pain & anger
Just a thought away.
I'm constantly fighting me
To keep my mind at ease.
God please
Just give me a drop
Of Your peace.

I guess that's why
They're called scars.
Because they never fully
Go away...

#saveme

Why, my soul, are you downcast?
Why so disturbed within me?
Put your hope in God,
for I will yet praise him,
my Savior and my God.
-Psalm 43:5

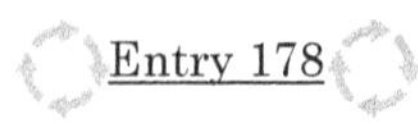

Entry 178

I feel uncomfortable
Everywhere.
My body
Covered in sores.
My heart aching.
Why is it that
I can feel the pain
Yet want to do nothing major
To change it?
This relationship
May be causing me discord
In all parts
Of my body.
But I don't wanna say goodbye.
Sometimes I feel like I love you
More than Christ.
When God says let go
I battle–
Him or you?

That's how I know
I must let it go.

But I don't know how...
How do you stop loving
The very person you love
With every breath you have?
Loving with an aching love.
A painful love.

Which symbolizes the fact
That it's strong.
...Right?
Because I'm willing to suffer for you.
I am suffering with you...

But really I believe
Most times I'm the only one
Suffering for this.
Fighting so hard
To truly heal this.

I have to start all over again.
With someone else?
Ugh.
Maybe the new person
Will have an impeccable work ethic.
Maybe with the same amount
Of effort I've given.
Yeah...
Maybe we'll be farther along
In less time
Because it'll be two that's working.
Not just one.

I'm stuck between
"Starting over could be so good"
&
"Starting over's gonna hurt so bad."

I don't know
What I'm doing.
All I know is
What I feel.
& I feel fear.
Anxiety.
Sadness.

Emptied...

The truth is
I know this is probably not
The best for me.
But I hope...

Truth fade away.
Truth clear as day.
I'm beginning to turn grey.
Beginning to lose breath in my airway.
Self-betray.
Holy Spirit, please pray.

In the same way, the Spirit helps us in our weakness. We do not know what we ought to pray for, but the Spirit himself intercedes for us through wordless groans.

-Romans 8:26

Entry 179

Everything I see
Reminds me
Of you.
I wish I could
Go through this world
With my eyes closed
For eternity.
So sick of drowning
In these sorrows.
Flashbacks.
Mind is froze.
The unforgettable moments
We chose to lead.
Whether my eyes are opened
Or closed
That's all I see.
I push this plate away
From me.
Because Love is no longer
Being served.

#Sick&Tired

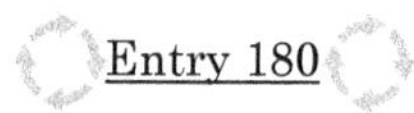

Entry 180

Searching the past
For a redemption
That only comes
Through Christ...

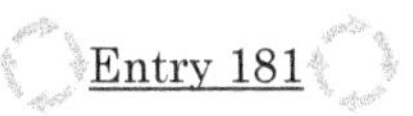

Entry 181

My mind wants to be sad
Because yesterday we said goodbye
Face-to-face.
But the truth I've denied myself
For months now
Is that we left each other
A long time ago.

Yesterday was the
Natural manifestation
Of what happened
In the Spirit
Long ago.
It always takes us
Humans time
To catch up
& courageously confront
What we've already been feeling
In our bodies
In our hearts
& in that small space
Way back in our brains
Where we tucked the truth away...

#NothingNewReallyHappened

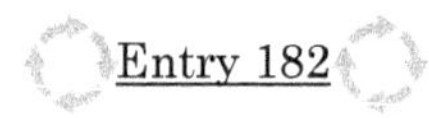

<u>Entry 182</u>

Can't save nobody
Who don't wanna be free

Fighting for you
More than I'm fighting for me

How am I confused
About the fact that
I'm drowning?

#misplacedenergy

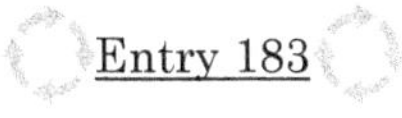

Entry 183

God
Thank You
For doing what
I wouldn't.
Thank You
For doing what
I couldn't.
Commanding me
To let go of
What had already
Been ruined...

And I will ask the Father, and he will give you another advocate to help you and be with you forever—the Spirit of truth. The world cannot accept him, because it neither sees him nor knows him. But you know him, for he lives with you and will be in you.

-John 14:16-17

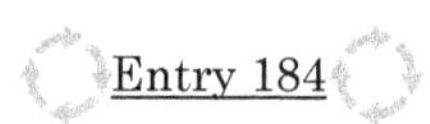

Entry 184

Christ keeps it at bay
But it never goes away.
So you gotta tap in
To His Spirit every day.

#DailyRestoration

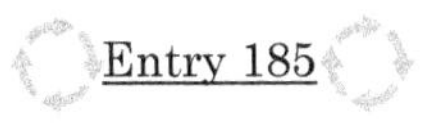

Entry 185

Highs & lows.
You really gotta *feel* it
to *understand* it.

What pain produces in me
is unmatched art.
God has to pain me
in order to pull
His treasure out.
I can't just sit
& say ouch.
I have to really
feel the hurt
to understand
the feeling.
The broken.
His people.
The chosen.
People are in bondage.
I can't just answer God's call.
I have to *feel*
what He's talking about.
Oppression.
Abuse.
Discord.
Emptiness.

For many
this is their lives.
The only thing
they've ever known.

For me
it was just but
for a moment
because I know
who's on the Throne.
But I had to
& have to
walk through some stuff
to understand the oppression
of the people
God is calling me to deliver.

#CantGetThisWithoutThat

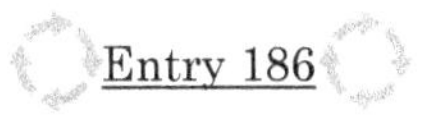

Entry 186

You passively pursued
To get me to disobey
& dishonor
The Savior of my life.
The very breath
In my lungs.

You never wanted me alive.
You wanted my flesh.
You wanted me dead.
Dead to real decision-making.
You coerced me until
I gave in to my flesh
& you stamped God's name
On it.

#misled

The priests did not ask,
'Where is the Lord?'
Those who deal with the law did not know me;
the leaders rebelled against me.
The prophets prophesied by Baal,
following worthless idols.
-Jeremiah 2:8

(Baal – the god of perversion & prostitution)

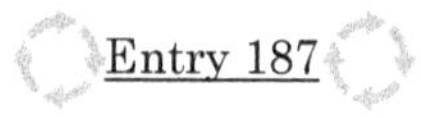

Entry 187

The water has an interesting way
Of freeing my mind
& allowing the wisdom gates
To open & flow.
Anytime I'm in distress
Or needing guidance
I go to the water
Where I'm most free.
I can sit in expectancy
That I will receive.

Thank You Holy Spirit
For meeting me by the sea.

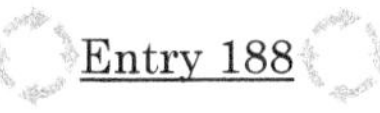

Entry 188

I've learned
That those with
The same soul
As me
Will understand my writing.
Even if it's jumbled up.
Here.
There.
& everywhere.
All I have to do
Is speak
From the heart.
True poets don't need
The preceding explanation
Or full sentences.
We understand
The chopped thoughts :)

See because the poets
Of this world
Are those who feel everything
Deeply.
I feel your pain.
I feel my pain.
I feel Mother Earth's pain.
It's all interconnected.

I cry your tears
& mine.
So even if
You cannot complete
Your thought…
I can.

My heart understands.
You are not alone.

Entry 189

It feels so good
To escape from them–
Those who linger heavily
In my past pain.
The responsibilities
Of work & family.
Maybe even the call
Of God.
I sit at the ocean
& I feel
I am home.
I say,
"God, I wanna stay here forever."
He says,
"Only for a little while.
Because they need you back there."

Peace is made for chaos.
One day I'll be home again.
Permanently.
Undeniably free.
For eternity.

#LivingSacrifice

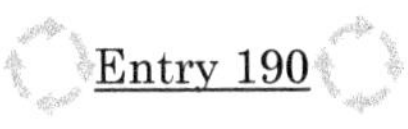

Entry 190

Once I left
It became easy
To exist

#Freedom

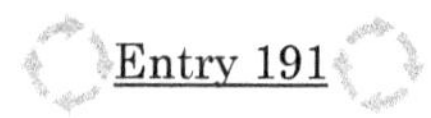

Entry 191

When I'm coming down
Off the rush
Of the day's high
Of busyness
I am reminded
Of how tender
My wounds still are...

#mentallytired
#tiredoffightingthesethoughts

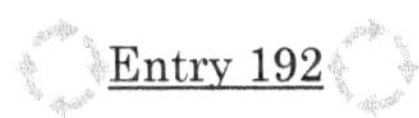

Entry 192

God,
Please heal my broken heart.
Please heal my broken confidence.
Please heal my broken trust.
Please heal me from what was...

-5am cries

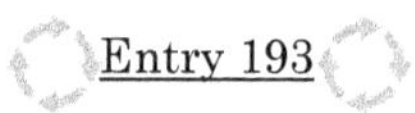

Entry 193

Every bit of emptiness in me
You will fill.
Every bit of brokenness in me
You will heal.

#iTrustYouLord

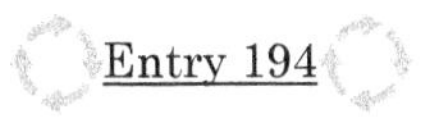

Entry 194

The kid in me
Wants to keep
Everything she gets
To avoid the hurtful
Experience of loss.
Even if
It's hurting me...

#hoarder

Entry 195

My life
Doesn't belong
To me.
When it did
I took it
Time & time again.
& God
Like a video game regenerator
Brought me back to life
Every single time.
So for the last time
He said to me,
"Hand Me the sticks."

With Him
I will lose my life.
But I will gain it.
& the old me
She'll repeatedly fight
To get back in the
Driver seat.
Thinking she knows
What's best for me.

She will kill me
Again & again
Without an end
& I will pretend
That it doesn't
Hurt me.
Becoming more solidified
In complacency.

The truth hurts
So freaking bad.
The truth strips.
The truth rips
Away at any & everything
In my path
That I've deemed
As my own.
Leaving me with
What feels like nothing...
Again...
I am empty.

But the truth saves...
As much as I
Don't wanna admit that
As truth.
I cannot deny
Its truth.

It saves me
From killing myself
Aimlessly.
God says
There will be a reward
For my slain life.
It's guaranteed.
& when it's time
For me to die again
I have to fight
The thoughts
That say
That's not true
Or enough...

Then Jesus said to his disciples, "Whoever wants to be my disciple must deny themselves and take up their cross and follow me. For whoever wants to save their life will lose it, but whoever loses their life for me will find it. What good will it be for someone to gain the whole world, yet forfeit their soul? Or what can anyone give in exchange for their soul?

-Matthew 16:24-26

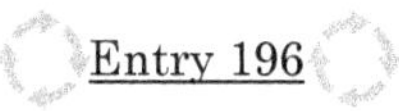

Entry 196

Death itself
Or death of self.
The constant thoughts
That influence
My behavior.
Suicide.
Or to die
For Christ.
The pressure
Is ever-present.
No matter the standpoint.
Kill the flesh or
Kill the Spirit.
Paul understood me best:

I do not understand what I do. For what I want to do I do not do, but what I hate I do. And if I do what I do not want to do, I agree that the law is good. As it is, it is no longer I myself who do it, but it is sin living in me. For I know that good itself does not dwell in me, that is, in my sinful nature. For I have the desire to do what is good, but I cannot carry it out. For I do not do the good I want to do, but the evil I do not want to do—this I keep on doing. Now if I do what I do not want to do, it is no longer I who do it, but it is sin living in me that does it.

So I find this law at work: Although I want to do good, evil is right there with me. For in my inner being I delight in God's law; but I see another law at work in me, waging war against the law of my mind and making me a prisoner of the law of sin at work within me. What a wretched man I am! Who will rescue me from this body that is subject to death? Thanks be to God, who delivers me through Jesus Christ our Lord!

So then, I myself in my mind am a slave to God's law, but in my sinful nature a slave to the law of sin.

-Romans 7:15-25

Entry 197

God's changing my story.
Thank You Jesus.
He's refining.
Thank You Jesus.
No more dying
To the life-giving assets
Jesus grants me.

Kill every part of me
That wants death itself.
Kill every part of me
That desires brokenness
& mess.

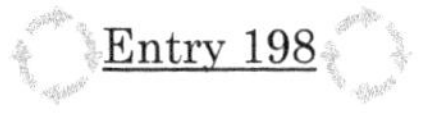

Entry 198

We're all addicted
To something
That kills the pain.
My addictions bounce
From men to friends.
Drugs & drinks.
To allowing my brain
To never cease to think
Negative thoughts.
Worrisome.
Past overload.
Overly blown.
At how this or that
Could happen.

Now it's coffee.
I get the jitters.
But I feel like
Nothing can stop me.
From moving.
Producing.
Distracting me
From what's happening
Internally.

Entry 199

My Spirit's flying.
Slowly but surely
I'm dying.
To self.
My dreams.
Visions.
Desires.
Light of the world?
Hmmm.
Wondering what
Lights it?
Everything in
My soul
Being set on fire.
Refining.
Redefining.
Rearranging.
Keeping me from the danger
My flesh so easily craves
& entangles with.
My flesh gravitates
Toward danger.
Pain.
& things that'll bring anger.
It's like somewhere
Subconsciously
I desire it
Because it's easier.
Familiar.

For the flesh desires what is contrary to the Spirit, and the Spirit what is contrary to the flesh. They are in conflict with each other, so that you are not to do whatever you want.

-Galatians 5:17

Entry 200

Don't wanna talk
but I want love & attention.

I'm feeling empty.

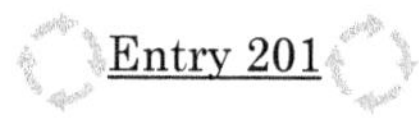

Entry 201

He wants me

:)

But he doesn't deserve me

:(

Entry 202

I want to be wanted
By you
But I feel this pain
Because I'm with you

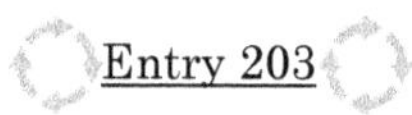

Entry 203

Thank You God
for beautiful skies
thick thighs
& kind guys

Entry 204

EMBRACING ME.

YOU BROKE ME.
BUT YOU HELPED MAKE ME.
THANK YOU...

Entry 205

My soul got so many scars.
You can't see any of them
In my face.
What a gift God gave me.
This pretty face.
But most times I envy it.
It's like a natural mask.
People see me
But they don't really see *me*.
They see pretty.
Not realizing how much
Pretty hurts.
I'm broken inside.
Yet all you see is this face
I didn't even ask for...
I didn't even choose...
It's just here.
Existing on me.
The real me–
This heavy soul
Who overthinks.
Dwells on anxieties.
& Cries regularly.
I'm screaming
But nobody hears me.
They just see my pretty face
& insist that I'm okay.

Like pretty people
Don't have real problems
To face...
I'll be damned.
I'm sure I have more problems
Than most.
Because I get taken advantage of
As a result of this pretty face.
People don't *really* see me.
They see an image.
A role.
A life.
With this face.
But they don't really see me!
My heart.
My desires.
My needs...
& that hurts.
Sometimes I wish
They could really just
Look within me
& see
What I see.

#lonely

Charm is deceptive, and beauty is fleeting;
but a woman who fears the Lord is to be praised.
Honor her for all that her hands have done,
and let her works bring her praise at the city gate.
-Proverbs 31:30-31

Entry 206

My soul shivers
At the demons
Of depression
Self-loathing
& exhaustion
All hovering over me.
Working hard to
Overcome me
Successfully...
Yet my Spirit
Stands strong & boldly
Waiting to swoop in
& save the day.

:):

#ExistingInTheInBtwnOfTheDuality...

Tears streaming down
My face.
Wanting to give up
& give in
to my final breath.
“I’m tired,”
I cry to myself.

But something else
In me won’t let me
Cower over
& die.

"It gets better.
It always gets better with time,"
Comes out my lips.
But I know for sure
It comes from
A different Source...

Thank You God
For responding expeditiously
To my cries
In the dark quiet
Lonely night.

I am reminded that
I'm never alone...

I will exalt you, Lord,
for you lifted me out of the depths
and did not let my enemies gloat over me.
Lord my God, I called to you for help,
and you healed me.
You, Lord, brought me up from the realm of the dead;
you spared me from going down to the pit.
-Psalm 30:1-3

Entry 207

It's all for
Your glory
& our growth
& to experience
Your goodness

Entry 208

You caused me to lose you.
How selfish of you.
I thought I'd have forever
With you.
You don't love me.
You don't even love yourself.
No matter how much
Of a facade
You waltz around wearing.
You don't care
About anybody
But yourself.
You're such a wreck.
You wrecked me!!
I wish our worlds
Never collided
With such a brutal bang.
I wish we could take back
Every idle decision made
Against God in vain.
Because today we pay.
& since I left you
It continues to rain.
Some days it lets up.
But it never fails
To come back
& visit again...

#IHateYou.

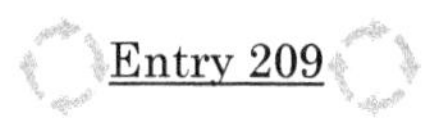

Entry 209

Jesus
Do You still cry
Over the crucifixion?
Do You still cry
About the pain
& rejection?
Or were Your deep sorrows
In Isaiah 53
Only for us?
Because I still cry over
What was...:/

Entry 210

Lord
Keep me in the know
Of what I need to know.
& what I don't
Help me to let it go.

#Wisdom&Boundaries
#LearningToLetYouLead
& #ProtectMeFromMyEnemies

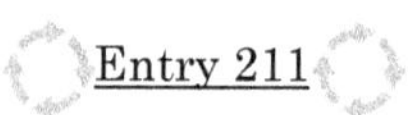

Entry 211

These looks
get old.
So tell me
what's in
ya soul?

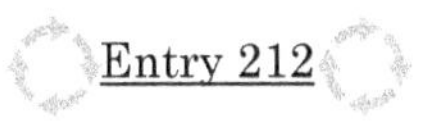

Entry 212

It's funny how
Deception works
Right?

Everything can feel
So right
Yet be all wrong.

Thank You God for
Seeing me.
Saving me.
Hearing the cries
Of my soul
As I forced myself
To cry silently.
Trying to appease.
Thank You God
For knowing
My heart's needs.
For not giving up
On my destiny.
For always exuding mercy
& always being a friend to me.

You are so divinely kind.

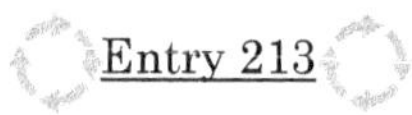

Entry 213

You are a big hug.
You are the gentle touches
Of a back rub.
You are the comfort
In the midst of heartache.
You are the smile of happiness
After months of depression.
You are the joy resurrected.

Entry 214

I've been through things.
A lot of things.
But I still have to be soft
Because that's what
God calls me to.
Because that's what saves me.
That's what keeps me free.
So excuse me
While I change my perspective
Of what happened to me.
Excuse me
While I learn new concepts
Of how to be.
While I smile & sing.
Even though those around me
Are unhappy & dying.
Of anger & hate.
I can smile
Because I choose to.
I can be joyful
Because I choose to.

It's just that simple.
It's just that hard.
It's just that liberating.

#I'mBreathingAgain

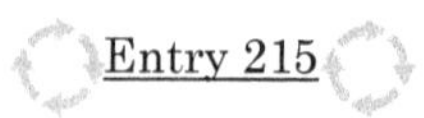

Entry 215

I look at my car
Parked
Alongside a truck
& think,
"That's how I feel."

Small.
In comparison to
Everything around me.

Insignificant.
Ineffective.

Like I'm just going through
The motions.
Like I'm the only one
With this level
Of devotion.

Is what I'm doing
Even changing anything?

Do I even have
The capacity
Or qualifications
To change a life?
These kids' lives?

Their issues
So massive.
Their spirits
So broken.

Who am I?

I'm new.
I'm young.
I'm little.
God are You sure
I'm the one?

Look at all the things
I've messed up
In my past.
Damn near every relationship
I've ever had.
I'm alone
With no real
Consistent friends.
Are You sure
I'm not the problem?
While You're calling me
To solve another one.
Are You sure this task
Isn't too far beyond me?

He responds,
"Yes it is.
That's why you have Me.
You are small.
But I am big.
Without Me
You *are* ineffective.
But every day
Every single day
You are desperately searching
For ways to empty yourself
& come to My well.

Maybe you aren't enough
For where I'm calling you.
But with Me
There's *nothing* you cannot do.

You are the chosen one
No matter what
You've been through.
Regardless of any mistakes
Or wrong paths you'll choose.

As long as you come back to Me
You'll be the one I use."

How priceless is your unfailing love, O God!
People take refuge in the shadow of your wings.
-Psalm 36:7

Entry 216

Isn't it amazing
How one can
Break your heart
& you can still
Love them
With all the little
Broken pieces?

Because we were made
In Love's image.
Made to Love.

Because we are Love.
No matter how much
Or what
We endure.
It always comes back to Love
With us humans.
Looking for the next one to Love
& lose ourselves in...

Entry 217

It's what's behind
Your breasts
That gets
What's in his chest

Entry 218

You've seen
My ugly
& you still
Love me

Thank You Christ

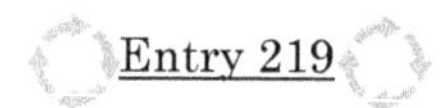

Entry 219

Your husband will never be
that missing piece
because what happens
when he dies?
You lose your hope?
Heck no!
God will not have that.

#GodFillsInOurBlankSpot

Entry 220

We're looking for something
to fill that hole.
That hole is gonna be there
every day
so that we consistently
pursue Jesus.
Nothing you get is gonna fill it
other than Jesus.

You are the "w" to my "hole."
Hole → Whole.

You complete me.

#WholeInYouAlone

But now thus says the LORD,
he who created you, O Jacob,
he who formed you, O Israel:
"Fear not, for I have redeemed you;
I have called you by name, you are mine.["]
-Isaiah 43:1 ESV

Entry 221

Constantly
I'm in my mind.
There's a whole world
Of things happening
In the in-between.
Fears & fallacies
Being challenged.
Challenging me.
I work endlessly
Cleansing my internal.
To keep my heart pink.
Throbbing.
Beating.
Purifying me.
Invading everything.
Formulating me.
Molding "we".
As long as I keep
My head in the clouds
Close to Christ
There is no obstacle
I cannot beat.
I am becoming
Yet simultaneously
I am free.

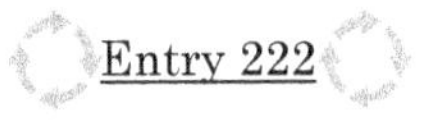

Entry 222

The severing.
Severely cutting me.
Over & over again.
Persistently.
Pessimistically.
Fighting to mold me.
I thought I left you.

Did you leave me?

Your thoughts–
They find me.
I'm getting over it.
Turning a new leaf.
Yet the thought of you
Keeps finding me.

Worship music blasting.
Truth is I'm struggling
To believe a thing
We're singing.

Does it ever go away?
The memories...
The thoughts of you?

I don't know how
I can survive
Living this way.

I thought I was free.
& then in comes
Another memory.
A familiar place
Or thing.
It always happens.
Every time.
Not just one time.
Not just a few times.
Every time.
Why the hell
Is there a fight
For my mind
Every single day?
I promise I never want
My flesh to win again.

I feel as though
I'm in-between two worlds–
The plaintive past
& this prized present.
Like my Husband
Trying to show me
How much He loves me
By showering me with Love
Kisses & gifts.
Yet for some reason
My past keeps knocking
At my door.

Slowly I drift.
& I'm split between
Being sad over what was
& being glad that I survived
& came out with a true Husband.
Being present with my real Lover.

For your Maker is your husband—
the Lord Almighty is his name—
the Holy One of Israel is your Redeemer;
he is called the God of all the earth.
-Isaiah 54:5

Entry 223

I'm stuck between
punishing myself
for my poor choices
& praising myself for exuding
this level of perseverance & commitment
to the overall goal
regardless of the feelings felt.

Wanting better
& more for myself.

Entry 224

I'm wrecked.
I know God can
& will bring me through this
Like He does everything else.
I just can't see it now.
I must trust.
Listen & hear
When I cannot see.
I don't know how
To get my flesh in check.
I always struggled
With this worthiness concept.
What if I always do?
I'm not even married
In the natural yet
& I keep pushing
My Husband away.
Going back to the past...
Relationships.
Remembering the pain.
I've always struggled with
Depression & getting stuck
In the pain of things...
Loss.

It's so comfortable
To lay there.
Being embraced
By this falsified version
Of comforting emotions.
Depression is big & fluffy.
A dark cloud.
A dark
Fluffy comforter.
I like the dark.
Because I'm going along
With them
I don't have to fight
My insecurities.
I cower over
Without a fight.

....

This isn't me.
I am a fighter.
I fight with the King.
I can't get tired.
Or if I do
I must tap Him in.
What happens if
I get tired & sin?
Then I'm back
At the beginning again.

If I'm not stretched
I don't fall.
I'm afraid of falling
& learning how to walk.
So I fall
& cowardly crawl.

Will I ever win this battle
Against depression?
My heart hurts for me.
God's heart cries for me.
My mind is tired.

I am a fighter.

We are hard pressed on every side, but not crushed; perplexed, but not in despair; persecuted, but not abandoned; struck down, but not destroyed.

-2 Corinthians 4:8-9

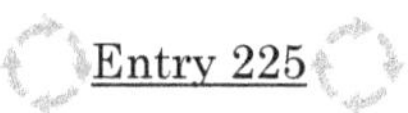

Entry 225

I just want Jesus & my man.
Jesus in my man.
Jesus, my man.
But Jesus, he's just a man...

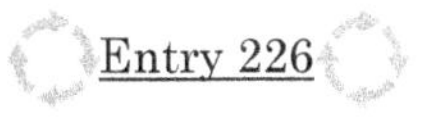

Entry 226

Sometimes
I just wanna
Run away.
I wanna run
Away from
The responsibilities
Of God.
& toward His comfort
& Love alone.

I'm so hard pressed.
I feel like
I can't breathe.
It's all coming
After me.
Down on me.
This past of sadness.
These desires
That keep me
Entertaining this madness.
I'm about to combust.
Tears piling up.
I look outside
The window
For a way
Of escape.
I thought it was over.
The heartache
When I forgave.

The toxicity-craves
When I went the other way.

The way my heart cries
For you.
Hidden deep within.
Defending this territory
As if it's his.

You steal my joy
& I allow it.
I'm tired of fighting
These feelings
With your name
Stamped on them.
Can't I just
Give them to you?
Pray that you'll do
What you need to.

No.
No I can't.
Because you have not a clue
What to do
With this tender heart
Of mine.

I tried.
I've tried.
I've died
& died.
I'm tired.

I've cried.
& even now
I can't stop crying.
With or without you.
My heart cries about you...
& me
& what used to be.
& some part of me
Can't seem to
Let it be.
Some part of me
Doesn't really wanna
Be free.
That's the only thing
I can come up with
Because as soon as I
Remove myself
From your clutch
I willingly walk back into it
& sit comfortably.
What is wrong with me?
Do I really want
Brokenness
Or the King?

These desires
Leave me tired...

The heart is deceitful above all things
and beyond cure.
Who can understand it?
-Jeremiah 17:9

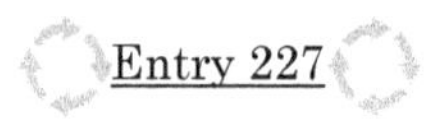

Entry 227

I have died.
I mourn me.
I mourn what was.

I am alive.
I am alive in Christ.

I died because I was in sin
Impurity & unholiness.
I live because I now follow
God's commands.
Which brings me life
Righteousness & peace.

To choose death or life?
I am both simultaneously.

–Self talks when I'm struggling to believe
I'm delivered & I've been set free...

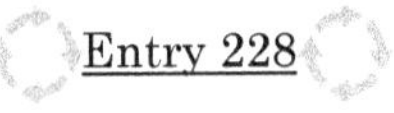

Entry 228

We only remember the pleasure
But please
Consider the whole picture

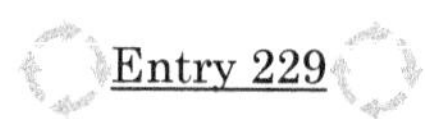

Entry 229

I come with a lot of
Baggage.
Attitude.
Feelings.
& You're still faithful
& committed to me.
& hopeful for me.

Thank You Jesus.

Entry 230

Appreciate the arts.
That's somebody's heart.

Entry 231

I really don't wanna be famous.
I just wanna be recognized for my heart.
My words of truth.
& my expression of feelings.

#DoYouHearMeNow

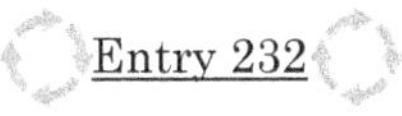

Entry 232

God told me,
"I forgive you
because I know
you were looking
for your dad
in him.
Looking to fill a hole
you never made.
I have mercy
because I know
your heart's intentions."

I've been looking for my dad forever.
Looking to fill a void.
In my heart.
With men.
Like him.
Running right into the trap of the enemy.
The heartbreak & chipping away
of my self-esteem, self-worth, self-image.
Hurting myself.
Not realizing.
& not knowing how to stop.

Holy Spirit revealed the truth to me this time around.
Never again will I be bound.

Moses answered the people, "Do not be afraid. Stand firm and you will see the deliverance the Lord will bring you today. The Egyptians you see today you will never see again.["]
-Exodus 14:13

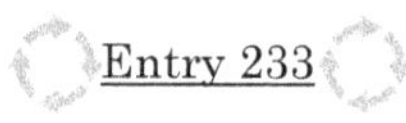

Entry 233

Losing you was the best thing
I could ever do.
Because it helped me see
That God's Love is really true.
No matter what I look like.
Regardless of what I do.
No matter what I choose.
God's Love is never removed.

And I am convinced that ***nothing*** *can ever separate us from God's love. Neither death nor life, neither angels nor demons, neither our fears for today nor our worries about tomorrow—not even the powers of hell can separate us from God's love. No power in the sky above or in the earth below—indeed, nothing in all creation will ever be able to separate us from the love of God that is revealed in Christ Jesus our Lord.*

-Romans 8:38-39 NLT (emphasis mine)

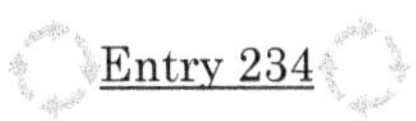

Entry 234

Holy Spirit
Thank You for being
The advocate
& sound mind
In my head
When I'm on
My last thread

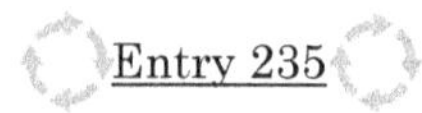

Entry 235

My friends
Encouraged me
To pick my own way
& not God's.
Even after verbalizing to them
This way of being
Is not God's Law.
Yet they continue to
Get in front of many people
& portray that they're letting God
Into *their* hearts.

#FirsthandExperiencesWithPharisees

"Woe to you, teachers of the law and Pharisees, you hypocrites! You are like whitewashed tombs, which look beautiful on the outside but on the inside are full of the bones of the dead and everything unclean. In the same way, on the outside you appear to people as righteous but on the inside you are full of hypocrisy and wickedness.["]

-Matthew 23:27-28

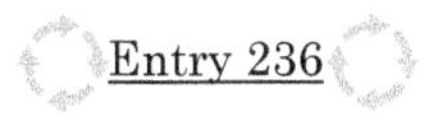

Entry 236

Now I'm beginning to see
they're men
just like me.
Ugly as can be
when we move
& don't allow
the Spirit to lead.
There is nothing
pretty to see.
That picture was fabricated.
Untrue.
I was deceived.

Now
I can handle the truth.

I am free.

To the Jews who had believed him, Jesus said,
"If you hold to my teaching, you are really my disciples.
Then you will know the truth, and the truth will set you free."
-John 8:31-32 (emphasis mine)

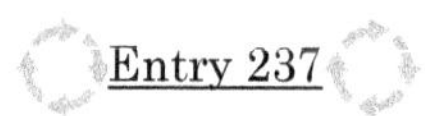

Entry 237

I thank You
for the privilege
to learn Love
in a new way

[challenging relationships]

Entry 238

You can write it down
but it's nothing like
the experience.

Entry 239

It's more than
about the prophecy
being accomplished.
It's about the process
being fully experienced.

God can prophesy
something to you.
Telling you
who you'll become
& what you'll do.

But as you're becoming–
what you'll lose
in mindsets
& perspective shifts
in those moments
of faith & peace development–
that's where some of
the most potent power resides.
It is in those moments
that we really change lives.

#MomentsCreateMovements

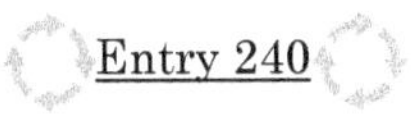

Entry 240

Will I always be misunderstood?
Is my capacity too much
For the world around me?
My depth & meticulousness
A rarity?
Where is my tribe?
I feel like I constantly cry.
I try.
I try.
I go here.
Pour there.
Hope here.
Invest there.
& come out having fed
Yet can take no one with me
To the next level or place.
I understand why
But maybe I don't.

Does understanding
Block out the feelings
Of despair & desire?
Emptiness?
Ever so often
God's cleaning out house
& the more I learn myself
My language gets weirder
& weirder.
Nobody understands what I am saying!!!!!!

I'm drowning
But she can't even see.
She doesn't understand
My sorrow & my needs.
She minimizes them.
Until soon
There'll be no more me.
Then would she be happy?
Having had silenced the truth.
The Holy.

What does it really mean
To be free?
Because this world straps me down
DAILY.
Will I ever TRULY be free?
OR should I expect that
As my reward "to be"?
Once I hear
"Well done My good & faithful
Imani"...

#weary

He was despised and rejected by mankind,
a man of suffering, and familiar with pain.
Like one from whom people hide their faces
he was despised, and we held him in low esteem.
-Isaiah 53:3

Entry 241

I seriously do not know what I am doing.
I am being suffocated.
Looking around
I see lives content
With mediocrity.
Walking zombies.
Hearts dead & off.
Am I the only one fighting
To keep my heart pumping?!!?
It's sickening.
God why did You strap me here
So firmly?
I feel like they're killing me.
Why can't I get away?
Cowardly escape the pain?
Am I running away?
I've always wanted to.
Longed for it since a teen.
Never feeling seen.
Not speaking my pain.
Because everyone wants to remain
In *lala* land.
A land of dysfunction.
No accountability.
Where do the good ones go?
& why do You have to disperse us
So far apart?

I feel like I'm the only person
On the cleanup crew
For this community's mess.
So much unaddressed!
Going from generation to generation.
Parents feeding children
Toxicity & yelling,
"Don't question what you're being fed!
At least you have something to eat!"
Just because you survived
Your generation
Doesn't mean it was okay.
What you're feeding
Isn't good for the soul!
It's killing us slow!

I'm sick of talking.
Redirecting.
To people who don't care
To be corrected.
It's hell living with people
Like this.

Depression comes fast.
A slippery slope.
Tank slowly emptying.
Hope.

How can I have hope in them?
I watch them move in their flesh
Effortlessly
& deny God when He speaks.
They don't wanna be changed.
Challenged.

What am I to do?
Lord I am tired
Of Your people...

I feel empty
Yet simultaneously
Filled with rage & sorrow.

For although they knew God, they neither glorified him as God nor gave thanks to him, but their thinking became futile and their foolish hearts were darkened. Although they claimed to be wise, they became fools and exchanged the glory of the immortal God for images made to look like a mortal human being and birds and animals and reptiles.

Therefore God gave them over in the sinful desires of their hearts to sexual impurity for the degrading of their bodies with one another. They exchanged the truth about God for a lie, and worshiped and served created things rather than the Creator—who is forever praised. Amen.

-Romans 1:21-25

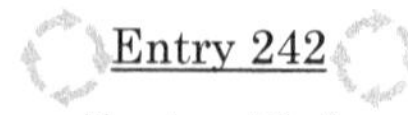

Entry 242

I'm terrified.
Terrified to hope again.
Terrified to open
My heart again.
To invest
Just to be rejected.
Misunderstood.
I'm terrified
To walk toward it
With an open heart
& with an expectation
Of good things
Because what happens to me
When it's left unfulfilled?
The only one brokenhearted
Distraught & left
With a disfigured heart
Is me...
It's easier not to hope big.
Less of me gets chipped away.
I DON'T KNOW HOW TO HANDLE LOSING PIECES OF ME!
I'm so scared!
I don't like this story!
I just wanna hide!
Tuck my head under the covers
Like the scared little girl I am.
Every word God has spoken
Slowly dissipates.
Nothing has my attention
But this enormous wave!

A year has passed
& so much has changed.
Yet the pain never seems
To fully fade.
Pressure.
Please alleviate!!
You want me to walk
Through another fire?!
& convince me
That I'll come out unscathed?
You promise me I'll never struggle
This way again.
All I can think about
& focus on
Is the pain.
Year 4 in this lane.
2018 I lost Rock to the game.
A month later them boys had
Twonnie slain.
2019 we in the streets screaming
Keykey's name.
Another murder.
Drugs & greed to blame.
2020 I started seeing things clearer
& lost my two best friends.
Exploitation & shame.
Now here we are
2021
& I'm back at square 1.

Heart attacks.
My heart is literally being attacked.
Demands on it
That cannot be met.
I know that You're with me.
But please tell me
Why is it all SO heavy?!
You said Your burden was light.
Help me.
Hurry.
I'm losing my fight.
Depression's around the corner.
Prowling...
Every time!
Ugh!!!!
Why do I have to carry this!?
Battle this!
Be confronted with this demon!
Who has my back?
Who can I tap in when I'm losing?
Who will be there to back me up
When my thoughts & words aren't enough?

I hate them for leaving me.
I hate them for not doing their part.
I hate them for not sacrificing as they should have
So that we could still be together.
God I know that You'll never leave
But I want more than just You
On my team.

I want them to understand & support me.
Not that You're not enough
& I'm not privileged.
But some part of me
Wants the company
Of man.
I don't know why.
You made me this way.
I tried so long
& so hard
To shut this part of me off
& now I feel like it's taking over
My life.

I can't afford to feel this lonely again.
With the wars I'm in, I'm really needing a friend.

#lonely&afraid

Yet it was the Lord's will to crush him and cause him to suffer,
and though the Lord makes his life an offering for sin,
he will see his offspring and prolong his days,
and the will of the Lord will prosper in his hand.
-Isaiah 53:10

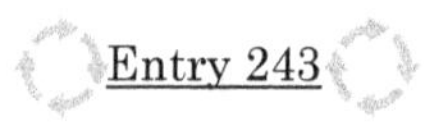

Entry 243

It's crazy how
It doesn't take much
To pull you right back in.

Into the discord
Brokenness
& chaos.

Be very careful
What you feed yourself.

Entry 244

Thank You for keeping me
When I didn't even wanna be kept

The LORD will protect you from all evil;
He will keep your soul.
-Psalm 121:7 NASB

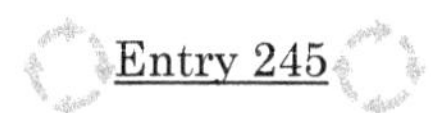

Entry 245

The general problem is
We wanna do for others
What we haven't even done
For ourselves.
What we aren't even willing
To do for ourselves most times.

What is that about?

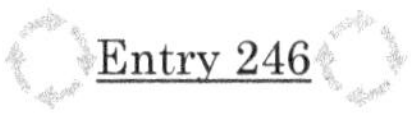

Entry 246

Stop envying other peoples' lives
& what you see
You don't know what price
They're paying for that
Ain't nothing free!

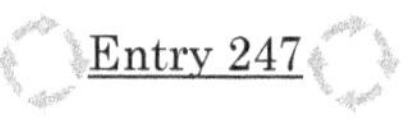

Entry 247

Just because they have it
doesn't mean they enjoy it

[unrighteous marriages]

"You shall not covet your neighbor's house. You shall not covet your neighbor's wife, or his male or female servant, his ox or donkey, or anything that belongs to your neighbor."
-Exodus 20:17

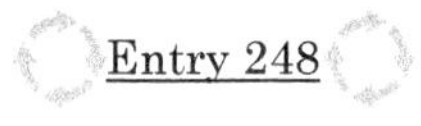

Entry 248

If I'm not talking
It's not because
I'm not feeling
Anything
It's because
I'm feeling everything
All too much

#mysilenceisLOUD

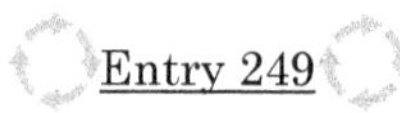

Entry 249

The thing is
you don't have to
live this way
& you choose to
for comfort
while ignoring
y(our) suffering.

So tired of living
under your reign.

Afterward Moses and Aaron went to Pharaoh and said, "This is what the LORD, the God of Israel, says: 'Let my people go, so that they may hold a festival to me in the wilderness.'" Pharaoh said, "Who is the LORD, that I should obey him and let Israel go? I do not know the LORD and I will not let Israel go."

-Exodus 5:1-2

Entry 250

She was naturally awkward & cringey
& I loved it because
I love authenticity

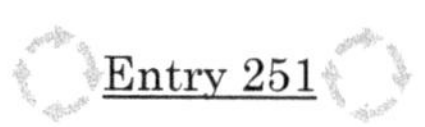

Entry 251

It's feeding a part of you
that wants to know
but is that what
you *really* want to grow?

Stop focusing on the darkness.
It'll grow.
& in your heart, you already know.

Entry 252

All that was sad girl behavior…

I'm healing now.
I'm calming down.
I can see Heaven in the mirror now.

(Thanks Jace)

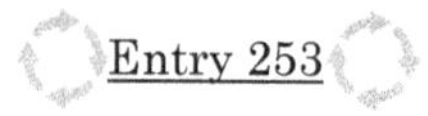

Entry 253

Heavy heart.
Heavy thoughts.
My mind is frozen in time.
Worried about things
that no longer matter.
Or *should* no longer matter.
But they still replay in my brain.
Resurface when I read my poems.
It happened.
It's over now.
Why do I consider it still?
The pain.
I guess the lessons never go away.
They shouldn't.
But in my life
in my mind
it feels as though
the pain sticks better
than the lessons.

May I have a brain exchange?

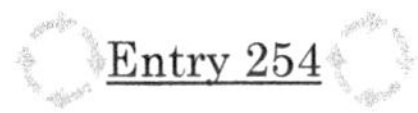

Entry 254

It's not easy
Or else everyone
Would be doing it.

That's what I think
When I'm processing
My emotions…

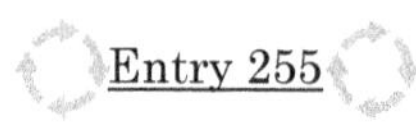

Entry 255

I was fragile then
That made me stronger

No longer seeking
The validation
& acceptance
Of man
The expensive
Of that
Was far too high

Obviously, I'm not trying to win the approval of people, but of God.
If pleasing people were my goal, I would not be Christ's servant.
-Galatians 1:10 NLT

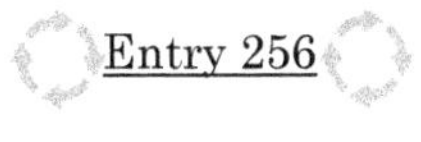

Entry 256

I'll never arrive
But
I can now say
I made it

Entry 257

It's amazing to be wanted by many
Yet sustained by none.
You watch men & *women*
Drool over me
So you think *I've* won.
I always end up alone
When it's all said & done.
Because in all reality
Within their hearts
They're numb.
They lust over me
& I'm not flattered.

#Protection&PurposeOverPleasure

Entry 258

If you walked in my shoes for a mile
You'd probably forget how to smile

I fight for my smile every day of my life.
That's why I follow Jesus Christ.
So that I don't lose my hope
In a world so hopeless.
So that I stay in a constant process
Of purification
In a world satisfied with deception.
If I didn't have Christ
I'd lose my mind
To the normalities of life.
Desires that set us on fire
For compromising things.
Unholy scenes.
Selfish ways of being.
I fight because there are kids
In this world who have yet
To see the Light.
Having been raised in a hell
That stole their innocence
Without regard for where
That tainted love
May lead them.
I fight for my smile.
I fight for my joy.
I fight for my Love.

Because even though
They are my birthrights
Through Christ
This world comes at me
From every angle
Every day
In every way
To steal what rightfully belongs to me.
These lips.
These cheeks.
The way my face creases
As my teeth align
With my heartbeat.

I am alive.

Entry 259

Everything was all fun & games.
But in that, I was the main accessory
to my own demise.
I think when you learn things like that–
The fact that *you're* the one killing yourself–
You begin to move a lot differently.
Certain fun ain't fun no more.
Certain songs don't hit the same.
Certain attention don't thrill you anymore.
It actually turns you off.
Because you now realize
you can lose your entire life
behind one connection that's not right.
Lacking *one* thing can stand between you
& manifesting *Life.*

Thank You Jesus
For Loving me enough
To tell me
What's right

Jesus looked at him and loved him. "One thing you lack," he said. "Go, sell everything you have and give to the poor, and you will have treasure in heaven. Then come, follow me."
-Mark 10:21 (emphasis mine)

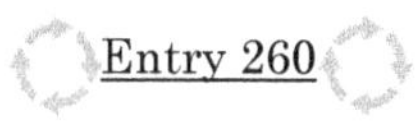

Entry 260

You *allowed* me
To find wisdom
In the wounds

There were times of despair
When I *couldn't* pray
Couldn't seek
Couldn't think

But somehow I've come out
On the other side
With wisdom
From those terrible times

Thank *You* for grace —
Undeserved favor.

You turned my wailing into dancing;
you removed my sackcloth and clothed me with joy,
that my heart may sing your praises and not be silent.
Lord my God, I will praise you forever.
-Psalm 30:11-12

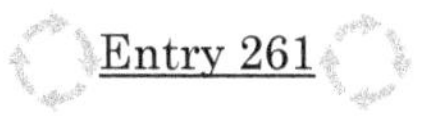

Entry 261

A lover of math
I'm constantly looking
For the formulas
In life…
Consistency.
To consistently
Ensure
Right
& success.

Life doesn't come with
Solidified formulas
Of existing.
Some things we simply
Have to experience.

Try & fall.
Fail & bawl.
Get it right
& ignite bliss.
Try it again
The same exact way
& make a mess.

There are no set
Formulas to life.
Some things
We just have to
Experience
& be acceptant

That it won't always
Feel good
Or be right.
That's the thing
About life.

God's goodness
Grace & mercy
Will be with us
Through it all.
Through every accomplishment
& every hard fall.

There are some things
You can only get
In the valley.
& some things
We are privileged
To feel
That can only be felt
At the mountaintop.

Maybe it is alright.
All right.
It's the balance
Of life.

Highs & lows.

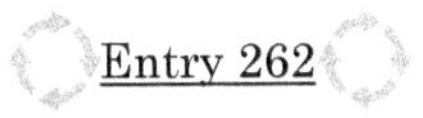

Entry 262

It's time.
Time to face yourself.
Face you.
Your ugly self.
Your insecure self.
Your needy self.
Your inner child.
AND
Your glorious self.
Your righteous self.
Your selfless self.
Your holy self.

You're renewed by the blood.
Both sides are worthy of His Love.
Don't fear facing you.
Don't doubt being renewed. ♡

Therefore, if anyone is in Christ, he is a new creation; old things have passed away; behold, all things have become new.
-2 Corinthians 5:17 NKJV

About the Author

Imani Gillespie was born and raised in Melbourne, Florida, an urban area swamped with much darkness and defeat. Drugs, violence, and fatherless households were a normality for her as a child. As she got older, limited perspectives and anger guided her behavior. Soon enough, while a teenager, she began to reap from those taught behaviors.

This book is a journey inside the heart of Imani, learning how to become who God has created her to be, while struggling to be free in her mind from the life she's always led; the life she had been trained to accept.

In *Heartbreak & Restoration*, Imani communicates messy feelings that come with succumbing to the flesh. She transparently addresses the madness that consumes her mind in these times; and yet, she also acknowledges how God has become an anchor of hope for her as seasons shifted from extreme to extreme. Through the text, readers will see that as Imani grows in her faith, God reveals Himself more and more within the darkness she experiences. *He restores every heartache. He brings us back from every heartbreak that He didn't even create... if we allow Him to.*

Imani's main focus for releasing this book is to share her heart with her readers and remind them God can redeem *anything* and *anyone*. She encourages her audience to stay openhearted, vulnerable, and gentle no matter what this world throws at them. Love is the very thing breathing air into our lungs. Love is maintaining the beat of our heart and connecting us to the beautiful things we partake in, in the world around us. We need Love to thrive. So, don't ever give up on Love.

> *We have come to know and have believed the love which God has for us. God is love, and the one who remains in love remains in God, and God remains in him.*
>
> *-1 John 4:16 NASB*

Stay Connected

Instagram: @imanitheauthor

Facebook: Imani Gillespie

Email: imanitheauthor1122@gmail.com

www.ingramcontent.com/pod-product-compliance
Lightning Source LLC
Chambersburg PA
CBHW071426070526
44578CB00001B/13

* 9 7 8 1 9 5 3 2 4 1 3 1 3 *